Painting a Poem

Mary Baker Eddy and James F. Gilman
Illustrate *Christ and Christmas*

Painting a Poem

Mary Baker Eddy and James F. Gilman
Illustrate *Christ and Christmas*

The Christian Science Publishing Society
Boston, Massachusetts, U.S.A.

Other publications of interest:

Science and Health with Key to the Scriptures
by Mary Baker Eddy

Christ and Christmas
by Mary Baker Eddy

Publisher's Cataloging-in-Publication
(Provided by Quality Books, Inc.)

Painting a poem: Mary Baker Eddy and James F. Gilman illustrate
   Christ and Christmas. – 1st ed.
      p. cm.
      Includes index.
      Preassigned LCCN: 97-6729
      ISBN: 0-87510-370-7

   1. Eddy, Mary Baker, 1821-1910. Christ and Christmas—
Illustrations. 2. Gilman, James F.—Themes, motives. 3.
Illustration of books, Victorian. 4. Christian Science.

BX6941.C47 1997   289.52'022
                                   QBI97-2249

Authorized literature of
The First Church of Christ, Scientist

Printed in the United States of America

Twentieth-Century Biographers Series

*I*N THE CLOSING YEARS OF the twentieth century, there is a growing awareness that the hundred years since 1900 will have registered a magnitude and pace of change, in every aspect of human affairs, that probably exceeds any historic precedent. In political, social, and religious institutions and attitudes, the sciences and industry, in the arts, in how we communicate with each other, humanity has traveled light years in this century.

"Earth's actors," said the Founder of Christian Science, Mary Baker Eddy, "change earth's scenes...." As we look back over the landscape of this century, some towering figures emerge into view: political leaders, scientists and inventors, authors, artists and musicians, social and religious pioneers, industrialists, and many others who helped "change earth's scenes."

Mary Baker Eddy is regarded as a major religious figure of the twentieth century and as a notable example of the emergence of women in significant leadership roles. Although her book *Science and Health with Key to the Scriptures* was published in 1875, in 1992 it was recognized by the Women's National Book Association as one of the 75 major books by women whose words have changed the world. When Mrs. Eddy was inducted into the National Women's Hall of Fame in 1995, it was noted that she had made "an indelible mark on religion, medicine, and journalism."

Mrs. Eddy's works are visible today in virtually every country of the world: in church buildings, in Christian Science Reading Rooms, in the distribution of the newspaper and religious periodicals she established and their derivative broadcast forms, in the wide circulation of her own writings, and most important, in the way hundreds of thousands of people conduct their everyday lives.

Mrs. Eddy wrote only briefly about herself, in a short volume titled, *Retrospection and Introspection.* She discouraged personal adulation, clearly hoping that people would find her character and purpose in her own writings rather than in the biographic record. Yet, she came to see the need for an accurate account of her life and gave specific if possibly reluctant acquiescence in the year 1910 to the publishing of the first of the biographies—Sibyl Wilbur's *Mary Baker Eddy.*

As we near the close of a century that directly witnessed some of Mary Baker Eddy's major contributions, The Christian Science Publishing Society, the publishing arm of the church she established, has reexamined the church's obligations to future generations and centuries, in providing an appreciation and understanding of her remarkable career. The Publishing Society now welcomes the opportunity of publishing, and keeping in print, a major shelf of works on Mary Baker Eddy under the general series title: "Twentieth-Century Biographers Series."

Mrs. Eddy's career and works have stirred humanity in the twentieth century and will continue to do so. Perhaps an appropriate introduction for this series is captured in her statement, in the Preface to *Science and Health with Key to the Scriptures:* "The time for thinkers has come." In that spirit, this series of biographies by many different twentieth-century writers is offered to all those who, now and in the future, want to know more about this remarkable woman, her life, and her work.

— * —

After Mary Baker Eddy asked artist James F. Gilman to illustrate her poem *Christ and Christmas* in the spring of 1893, they worked together throughout the summer preparing the eleven charcoal and wash watercolor drawings. A Christian Scientist, James Gilman had come to Concord, New Hampshire, the previous November and had been writing to friends about meeting Mrs. Eddy and being entertained in her home. Several of these original letters still remain. He also wrote about his experiences illustrating Mrs. Eddy's poem. Many years later he pulled together the content of his letters and brief notes he'd made at the time, connecting them with memory's strands. The diary-like format of his reminiscence bears evidence of this after-the-fact composition, for days go by without an entry, and information is missing.

James Gilman met Mrs. Eddy in the early 1890s, near the midpoint between 1866, which she marks as the instance of her discovery of Christian Science, and 1910, when her *Poems* was published. He presents a contemporary view of Mrs. Eddy at this specific time—the Christian Science movement was growing, spreading across oceans, yet her lifestyle remained extremely simple.

In the years after James Gilman's passing in 1929 several versions of his reminiscence were published. They were based on typed and revised copies of his writings, and as a result contained numerous errors. James Gilman's words in this volume are from his original handwritten letters, notes, and reminiscences—not fully available elsewhere. Care has been taken to accurately present what was said and done by Mary Baker Eddy and James F. Gilman during the process of illustrating *Christ and Christmas*. Records, letters, diaries, and other corroborative evidence in the Church History Department of The First Church of Christ, Scientist, in Boston, Massachusetts, were consulted. Discrepancies concerning the order of events and other details where memory was false have been corrected. Also some of James Gilman's personal musings did not speak to the topic of this book and so have been omitted.

In this book, after a brief section that sets the scene and one that provides information about James Gilman, are a collection of his letters about meeting Mrs. Eddy. Then, entries from his reminiscence have been interspersed with correspondence between Mrs. Eddy and him telling of their working together to illustrate *Christ and Christmas*. Reproductions of some of his art follow.

His capitalization is his own. Words he ascribes to Mrs. Eddy are, of course, filtered through his perception and memory or, as he wrote to a friend, "she did not use exactly these words but words amounting to the same." His accounts of the whys and wherefores are understandably subjective—and direct from his heart.

Contents

Mary Baker Eddy

Photo by S.A. Bowers

The Setting

CHRIST AND CHRISTMAS—
a poem illustrated with eleven mostly charcoal and wash drawings—was regarded by Mary Baker Eddy as one of her most important works. When a London newspaper asked her in 1907 what she considered her principal books, she listed six:

Science and Health with Key to the Scriptures
Miscellaneous Writings
Unity of Good
Church Manual
Christ and Christmas
Rudimental Divine Science

Christ and Christmas focuses on the advent of Christian Science. Mrs. Eddy wrote of it soon after its publication: " 'Christ and Christmas' voices Christian Science through song and object-lesson."[1] And she said of the illustrations that "these refer not to personality, but present the type and shadow of Truth's appearing in the womanhood as well as in the manhood of God, our divine Father and Mother."[2]

The artist was James Franklin Gilman, a landscape and portrait painter. As was common with many men and women of the time, James Gilman was quite a letter writer. During this period, he wrote long letters to friends about his first meetings with

Mrs. Eddy in 1892, his activities and surroundings. He wrote about illustrating the book, his work with Mrs. Eddy, his impressions of what he saw and heard, his struggles, his aspirations. Many years later he drew on these letters—along with sketchy notes made at the time, and his own memories—to create a reminiscence with diarylike entries. This after-the-fact compilation resulted in long vacancies in his account, as well as missing information, such as a Bible verse that was said to be important, but then was either not given or was vaguely described as "some Scriptural prophesy of Revelation."

It was an almost telephoneless time. Instead of picking up a phone or tapping out a message on a computer, Mrs. Eddy and James Gilman would write letters and notes to each other as the artwork on the book proceeded. Messages went through the mail or were delivered by hand. For *Painting a Poem,* letters and notes of Mrs. Eddy to Gilman, his letters to her, letters of his to friends, and selections from his compiled reminiscence have been arranged chronologically to give a picture of the project and the time.

Ever since the dramatic healing of near fatal injuries from a fall in Lynn, Massachusetts, in 1866—which she called "the falling apple that led me to the discovery how to be well myself, and how to make others so"[3]—she had dedicated her life to sharing this discovery. The years 1892 and 1893 were especially filled to overflowing for Mary Baker Eddy.

In 1891, two years before her collaboration with Gilman began, she had brought out a considerably revised and enlarged edition of her textbook of Christian Science, *Science and Health with Key to the Scriptures.* Some 21,780 copies of this book would be sold in 1893—a far cry from the first edition published in 1875 of one thousand books, a quantity which would last three years before the next reprinting. Early in 1893 Mrs. Eddy began working with her printer to produce the book on Bible paper, a paper difficult to obtain in the United States and difficult to run through the regular presses. She communicated to the printer: "It has always been my desire and expectation that my book should encourage more and more people to read the Bible."[4] She believed that having *Science and Health* similar in appearance to the Bible would aid students in using them together.

Her church, The Church of Christ, (Scientist), had been organized in 1879. Now, step by step—although not without opposition from some of her followers—she was reorganizing, moving it from a congregational model to governance by a self-perpetuating Board of Directors with rules and by-laws she would write for her church. A first step in this direction occurred in September 1892 when she executed a Deed of Trust giving land for a church in Boston to a Board of Directors. Later that month, at her request, twelve of her students met to formally organize The First Church of Christ, Scientist—The Mother Church.

The building of a Christian Science church edifice in Boston was a major concern for Mrs. Eddy. In the summer of 1892 she wrote in *The Christian Science Journal* an encouraging message to church members in which she said, "The First Church of Christ, Scientist, our prayer in stone, will be the prophecy fulfilled, the monument upreared, of Christian Science. It will speak to you of the Mother, and of your hearts' offering to her through whom was revealed to you God's all-power, all-presence, and all-science."[5] She asked the Board of Directors to begin construction in October 1893.

Filling offices with the right people was an ongoing duty. In

November 1892 she named a new editor of the *Journal,* and early in 1893 she appointed a new member of the Board of Directors, new publishers of her writings and of the *Journal,* and a new pastor of The Mother Church.

As always, Mrs. Eddy continued to correspond and meet with numerous students from all over the world, to write articles for the *Journal,* to encourage the growing number of local groups of Christian Scientists forming churches, and to battle opposition to the practice of Christian Science coming from the courts and legislatures. To one student facing court charges during this time, she wrote encouragingly, "Yes, my student, my Father is your Father; and He helps us most when help is most needed, for He is the ever-present help."[6] She closed her letter, "Write me when you need me. Error has no power but to destroy itself. It *cannot harm you;* it cannot stop the eternal currents of Truth." Her students often called her Mother,[7] and she did mother them and her Cause. In a long letter she sent to the First Church of Christ, Scientist, in Denver and published in the *Journal* in May 1892, she wrote what could describe all her activity and work: "...I, as a dictator, arbiter, or ruler, am not present; but I, as a mother whose heart pulsates with every throb of theirs for the welfare of her children, am present, and rejoice with them that rejoice."[8]

In 1893 she also helped her students prepare for the Christian Scientists' participation at the World's Parliament of Religions held in Chicago, as part of the huge Columbian Exposition, or World's Fair.

In these years Mrs. Eddy's staff was small: those she worked most closely with were a secretary, Calvin A. Frye; a housekeeper, Laura Sargent; a cook, Martha Morgan; and a laundress, Theresa Gegne. Another member of the household, E. J. Foster

Eddy, her adopted son, would visit—usually on weekends—from his base in Boston, where his major duty at the time was publishing *Science and Health.* (In the next few years, a self-indulgent temperament would carry him from the center of the Christian Science movement and eventually away from Christian Science itself.)

Added to everything else, Mrs. Eddy had moved in the summer of 1892 into her new home—a comfortably remodeled farmhouse on the outskirts of Concord, New Hampshire. It was a home in development. Work would continue for the next few years: the building of barns and other outbuildings, the planting of trees, shrubbery, berry patches, and flowers, as well as of orchards and fields of grain.

Into the midst of all this activity, in November 1892, James Franklin Gilman moved from Montpelier, Vermont, to Concord. Interested in Christian Science since 1884, he knew people who had studied with Mrs. Eddy, and he had met her adopted son when Foster Eddy stayed in Vermont earlier.

In March 1893, Mrs. Eddy proposed that James Gilman illustrate a poem she had written—*Christ and Christmas.* Although he would work primarily in charcoal and wash, the resulting drawings are actually executed in mixed media, for he also used pen and ink, and pencil. Published on December 2 that year, the book would even go back to press, before Mrs. Eddy withdrew it from circulation in January 1894. It would be reissued in 1897.

The letters and memoirs here reveal a work-in-progress—verses of the poem are moved, lines are changed, and ideas for the art are modified. (Even after the original publication, small changes were made in two of the drawings and the last one was completely replaced.)

Little of Mrs. Eddy's busy life, of the challenges facing her, appear in *Painting a Poem.* An account of one activity with one person, this is a narrowly focused, pinpoint view. But in this one man's experience and observations can be seen something of Mrs. Eddy's love, friendship, and motherliness. It is like a microcosm of her endeavors with so many students and followers; they are committed and striving, but not as committed as she, and not as awake to the things of the Spirit.

An inscription appears at the end of *Christ and Christmas:*

> Mary Baker Eddy
> and
> James F. Gilman
> Artists

This indicates her major role in delineating what should be illustrated and in further developing in the pictures the meaning of the verses they illustrate. Revealing something of their work together, she wrote: "I insisted upon placing the serpent behind the woman in the picture 'Seeking and Finding.' My artist at the easel objected, as he often did, to my sense of Soul's expression through the brush; but, as usual, he finally yielded."[9] Explaining the snake, she quotes from the Rotherham translation of the Bible a verse from the twelfth chapter of Revelation: "And the serpent cast out of his mouth, *behind* the woman, water as a river, that he might cause her to be river-borne."

The illustrations of *Christ and Christmas* are important. Their content is not incidental. For example, a major element in the art—present or absent—is the seven-pointed star, which does more than provide natural light. In her writing Mrs. Eddy often uses the star as a metaphor as when she wrote in a Christmas message: "The star of Bethlehem is the star of Boston, high in the zenith of Truth's domain, that looketh down on the long night of human beliefs, to pierce the darkness and melt into dawn."[10]

Two of the rectangular pictures are without the star or its light; "Treating the Sick" (where the bed is huge, the patient asleep, and the book closed) and "Christmas Eve" (which doesn't even have a star atop its holiday tree) are scenes where materialism predominates. In "Christmas Eve," no one, young or old, smiles; illness and debility are outlined, and behind the actors of the present lurk the shadowy figures of the past.

Two drawings are not rectangular—the oval "Christmas Morn" in which one angel appears to pray and the other to watch, a single tree stands tall in the landscape, and twelve sheep dot the hillside; and the completed circle of "Christian Unity."

The star shines fully on Jesus raising the dead in "Christ Healing," the woman poring over the Bible in "Seeking and Finding," the woman healing the sick man in "Christian Science Healing," the child reading *Science and Health* in "I thank thee O father...," the pair in "Christian Unity," the messenger in "Truth *versus* Error," and the victorious path from cross to crown in "The Way."

In June 1893, at a time when completing the art seemed mired, Mrs. Eddy told overnight guests about the book. Wrote one, "She spoke at this time with ardor of her work on her illustrated poem, *Christ and Christmas*. It was evidently dear to her heart."[11]

Soon after the book was published, Mrs. Eddy described it as "hopelessly original,"[12] and memorably she wrote to a young Christian Scientist in New York: "The Christ and Christmas was an inspiration from beginning to end.... If ever God sends you to me again I will name some of the marvelous guidances that He gave me. He taught me that the art of C.S. has come through inspiration the same as its Science has."[13]

James F. Gilman
A studio photograph taken in Gardner, Massachusetts, and given to
The Mother Church by Homer L. Hadley, Mr. Gilman's nephew

James F. Gilman

"MY PRECIOUS ARTIST," Mary Baker Eddy began one of her letters to James F. Gilman, and she closed it, "with deep love, Mother," a term she and her followers used in the 1890s.

Throughout their relationship runs a warm strain of filial and maternal affection. When they met, Mrs. Eddy had but recently moved into Pleasant View, her home in Concord, New Hampshire. Gilman had been an artist in and around Montpelier and Barre, Vermont, from the early 1870s, but his increasing study and practice of Christian Science led him in late 1892 to leave his work there and go to Concord, as he put it, "in obedience solely to his spiritual intuition that it would be spiritually good for him to do so." He would stay just over a year, until he moved to Gardner, Massachusetts, in February 1894.

Born in 1850, Gilman was about the age of Mrs. Eddy's son, George Washington Glover, and her adopted son, E. J. Foster Eddy. And his own mother, whom he described as "earnestly Christian," had passed on when he was ten years old.

James Franklin Gilman, like Mary Baker Eddy, grew up in a God-fearing Congregational home. As one early writer described that environment in Gilman's childhood town: "Every day the scriptures were read and God worshipped and not a child or servant suffered to grow up without being instructed in the principles of religion and taught to reverence the day, the word, and the name of God. [They] observed with great strictness and veneration the Christian Sabbath… some of them having traveled on foot two, three, or five miles to Woburn, as was the case with those living at Burlington and Wilmington. Some from the latter place used to travel on snow shoes, getting to Woburn between 8 and 9 o'clock in the morning and home about dark."[1]

Woburn, Massachusetts, the town where James Gilman grew up, was settled early in the 1600s, one of those first Puritan settlements in the New World. Around the end of the nineteenth century a citizen of the town, looking back to the early to mid 1800s, feelingly wrote of it, "The reputation of Woburn was so fair, the facilities for a comfortable livelihood so good that people from other places were attracted there and made this their home and found it for their advantage to remain in the then quiet town." Speaking of those years he wrote, "The shoemaker's shop, we often see attached to houses, or near them, is indeed a very necessary appendage, as a huge portion of the people hereabouts obtain a livelihood by shoemaking, and think it no disgrace to give their children this trade."[2] As those described, James Gilman's father was a shoemaker, crafting women's fine shoes.

When his mother passed on, Gilman's two sisters went to live with relatives of his mother in Vermont, and he and his brother stayed with others in the Woburn area. Of his start in making a living as an artist, he says:

In order to break the seeming limitations of his outward circumstances which appeared to bar his way to ideal unfoldment and to forbid education along usual academic training, he found himself ready to accept joyfully, at the age of twenty, a simple, humble way that was then presented to him through the kindly impulse of a neighbor, who, knowing of his exceptional capacity for drawing, offered to pay him if he would make for him a good pencil drawing of his home place....

An interest in the young artist naturally grew as a fruit of this first effort from nature in his rural home town through the seeing of his work, and later of other neighbors' home places, and, reaching out as it did into neighboring townships, supplied for a time the art-practice opportunities requisite for its self-supporting continuance.

It appeared to require in its earlier years much homeless roving in different townships and always a lone application to the naturally gradual mastery of technical difficulties, without other than self-instruction.

Gilman's first known piece of art depicts a scene in Wilmington, a community adjacent to Woburn. After a few years of executing mostly pencil and watercolor pieces in towns north and west of Woburn, Gilman moved to central Vermont. An aunt, who had taken in one of Gilman's sisters when their mother died, lived south of Montpelier, the state capital, for a time. Gilman began practicing his art around Montpelier and nearby Barre.

"Montpelier, Vermont"

In the summer he would remove to prosperous farms in the immediate area and paint portraits of the inhabitants and panoramic views of the home places. In these wide-ranging views, filled with rich fields and open skies, can be seen the people who lived there, working and playing, visiting and riding in their carriages—happy with their land and with their lot. In the corner of one pencil sketch, he placed the artist—himself—sitting high on a bluff under a tree with his sketch pad on his knees. In distant views he sometimes put features, such as animals in a barn, that could only be seen with a magnifying glass.

An affable, gentle man, he was remarked upon for his intelligence and kindness. One person who knew him later said that he had "a friendly disposition," that he was "a mild man who never used coarse or abusive language." Another said he was "scrupulously clean, and one who loved people, especially children."[3]

For part of the eighteen years or so that he lived in central Vermont, he had a studio above a bookstore in downtown Montpelier. Some of the time a men's literary society, The Apollo Club, met there. The bookstore downstairs, owned by a friend, was also a favorite haunt. In the winter when art commissions were slow and money was low, Gilman occasionally moved from his boardinghouse or hotel and slept in a room at the back of his friend's store.

Around 1886 he taught for several years at Goddard Academy in Barre, taking his students outdoors to sketch trees and streams and cloud-filled skies. He also gave private lessons.

One of the watercolors that Gilman made during his time in

"Winter's Day in Montpelier, Vt." as viewed from James F. Gilman's studio. He roomed sometimes in the Riverside House, the building on the left.

Vermont was of a friend, William Clark, as he worked on his farm near Barre. Clark, who had been a schoolteacher, had been wounded during the Civil War. Healed in Christian Science of the effects of those wounds, he attended one of Mrs. Eddy's classes at the Massachusetts Metaphysical College in Boston in 1888. Gilman himself had begun to study Christian Science in 1884.[4]

In 1893, at the time he was working on the illustrations for *Christ and Christmas,* Gilman wrote in the little leather-bound notebook he carried in his pocket, "If we really desire to understand Truth and grow, we shall find ourselves each day sincerely asking, 'What cross—that is what exercise of self-denial—may I bear today for the sake of the eternal good?' " It was a lifelong endeavor.

James Gilman wanted to be a Christian Science practitioner, a healer; he healed himself when he was in Vermont, took patients when in Concord, and he talked with Mrs. Eddy about Christian Science practice and his desires in that direction. Once he had moved to Gardner, Massachusetts, he continued his work as an artist, but he also announced in the local newspaper office hours as a healer. From 1900 to 1905, he advertised as a practitioner in *The Christian Science Journal.* By then he had moved from Gardner to nearby Athol, and there he helped to organize a Christian Science branch church and served it as First Reader. Several of his articles were also published in *The Christian Science Journal.*

In 1905 Gilman returned to his artwork, painting scenes around Gardner, Athol, Orange, and New Salem. In one of his views of the lovely common at New Salem, he painted himself sitting on a park bench reading a newspaper. For the 150th anniversary of Athol in 1912, he made a series of paintings of historical places associated with the city.

Although many of James Gilman's works remain in private hands, there are collections in the various areas where he spent considerable time. His art can be seen at the Vermont Historical Society in Barre and the Historical Society and the Public Library in Athol, Massachusetts, and the Swift River Valley Historical Society in New Salem, Massachusetts. The First Church of Christ, Scientist, in Boston, Massachusetts, also has a collection of his work, which includes—in addition to the original drawings for *Christ and Christmas*—pieces completed both in Vermont and the Gardner region of Massachusetts.

A man who was described by one critic as having "an affectionate tenderness for his subject,"[5] Gilman spent his last years in a quiet home near Boston. Although in the 1920s he withdrew his membership in The Mother Church, he quickly asked for it to be reinstated. To the end he remained faithful to the teachings he loved and the Leader he had fondly called Mother.

The opening of one of James F. Gilman's letters.
See pages 24–35 for the full text.

The end of the letter to Carrie Huse that James Gilman began
on December 18, 1892. See pages 17–24 for the full text.

"You see I am now in Concord, N.H."

Letters

Concord, N.H.
Dec. 18, 1892

Dear Friend Carrie.[1]

You see I am now in Concord, N.H. I have been here three weeks tomorrow. My first week here was mostly spent in finishing up two pictures that I failed to find time to finish before Thanksgiving in Waitsfield so I took my sketches along with me.

I am now at work in making a group of pictures of Mrs. Eddy's house and grounds for her photographer here, from which I suppose photographs will be made and sent to any ordering. The photographer is having the picture made as a present to Mrs. Eddy.

There are four views of the house and grounds and one view of Concord from the grounds. I thought when I came here that I should do something of that kind for Mrs. Eddy or Dr. Foster Eddy,[2] but he was called to Boston three or four days after I arrived here and has been there ever since.

I saw him the day I came at Mrs. Otis',[3] the practicing Christian Scientist here. He alluded to the desire of Mrs. Eddy for some pictures and said they had thought that next summer would be the time for some outside views of the place or from the place. He also said that, "Mother has asked me to have a good picture of myself made and perhaps I shall be able to attend to that now." He said he would see me in a few days, but he went to Boston before I saw him again. I was debating what I better do: go to canvassing for some work about here to be kept busy upon until the Dr.'s uncertain return or change my occupation and try to get into something a little more steady and reliable than art work, with myself as manager, when Mrs. Otis suggested that I ask Mr. Bowers[4] (Mrs. Eddy's photographer) if he hadn't some work in my line he would like done. He thought it over during the night and in the morning he had concluded he would have a picture made of Mrs. Eddy's house and grounds as before described. He had already had a picture made by a poor artist, photographs of which had been made but which none who had seen the place liked. You see the artist allowed himself to be governed by his own ideal and traditions about art more than by the actual appearance of the place before him and I don't wonder that they did not like it.

I had a splendid day for making the sketches, for December, and I ought to get some splendid pictures, for the scenery is beautiful, and I have no doubt but that I shall. I will send you the photograph when we get it. I have not seen Mrs. Eddy nearby or to speak with, but while I was sketching the house, she was driven up to her door and I heard her talking to the horses and suppose I saw her on the verandah. I was twenty-five or thirty rods[5] away.

I also saw one whom I suppose to be her, yesterday, while up there to get a few additional points that I failed to get while sketching the first time, and as it made a deep impression upon me, I will describe it to you. I was sketching some details of the house from the rear, at the lower end of the grounds, some sixty rods away from it, when a *dark* figure came out upon the upper verandah (there are three of them the full length of the house and ell on the south and rear side of the house) and began to walk the length of the verandah and back. I was there sketching some fifteen minutes or more and the black figure walked vigorously back and forth the length of the piazza and return, constantly.

Getting through with my sketching, my only way to the road led by the house and as I came nearer the house, the figure of course grew more distinct to my view as I occasionally glanced up, while the impressiveness of the blackness, *as blackness* grew upon my sense also. Coming quite close to the building, a couple of rods from it, I thought I would give the figure one last glance, and as I did so I noticed the fashion of the garb, that it was very peculiar, particularly the bonnet, or hat, which was large in size in proportion to the figure, which looked very short and small. The hat was so large and bent so around the head that no face was visible to me, although no veil was worn, and the depth of the black to my sense seemed beyond description and left an impression upon my mind of sackcloth and ashes as the Bible hints, or has it, that exceeded all my former conception of it. The verandah led from Mrs. Eddy's room, from which the figure first came, hence I suppose it to be the figure of Mrs. Eddy.

Perhaps my imagination magnifies, but it seemed to me the Founder of Christian Science was thus typifying in outward appearance the inner throes of anguish, perhaps habitually bourn, bourn that the immortal Life might appear to humanity as a demonstrated actuality, to the vanquishment of death in the proof to a world in the darkness of the innumerable woes of material sense that its woes, death included, was but a nightmare of illusion. Is it by such patient endurance of the woes of sin, not hers, that the world is shown its way to the kingdom of Harmony and Life eternal which is thus to become its salvation? It seems to me it is verily so, and this while so many of us who follow are asleep, comparatively. Seeing the figure as I did gave me a weird feeling such as I have sometimes felt in dreams, but not in waking hours. It has suggestions of work for me that I trust will find expression in appropriate action.

The Cause here has a good and wise representative in the person of Mrs. Otis, who was a primary student of Mrs. Eddy in 1886. Mrs. Eddy has since authorized her to teach and she has taught some classes in the year or more past. We have meetings every sabbath, open in a *quiet* way, to the public, and every Thursday evening to her students. I feel that I am now enjoying rare privileges. They have welcomed me here very kindly. It was Mrs. Otis who first suggested that I call upon Mr. Bowers, the photographer, to see if he did not need my services in some way. Making this picture of Mrs. Eddy's place for him is much better all around I think than it would have been to have made it for Mrs. Eddy direct. At the meeting there is generally an attendance of twenty-five or thirty.

Truly your friend,
James F. Gilman

Tuesday evening
Dec. 20, 1892

I kept this letter yesterday to see if what I had written of Mrs. Eddy in *black* on the rear verandah would keep over one day, and last night a young Scientist coming from Mrs. Otis' room

brought me word from her that Dr. Foster Eddy had returned
from Boston, and that I better go up and see him in the morn-
ing at Mrs. Eddy's house. Mrs. Otis has been desiring that I
should see Mrs. Eddy to talk with her, and I think that if I
called there when the Dr. was there, that he would take his
mother in and introduce me.

After seeing Mrs. Otis this morning, I decided to go up there
(the house is about a mile and a half west from the business por-
tion of Concord and is in the farming country), and after seeing
the Dr. a little he went out, as I supposed to see Mr. Frye[6] about
some plan drawings of the stone gateway to the grounds which
is to be in the picture I am making. Pretty soon he came back
with Mrs. Eddy, a small, bright, graceful appearing woman of
sixty or sixty-five,[7] with white hair, with a small slender, delicate
hand with which she greeted me at the introduction.

After referring to the wonderfully fine weather we are having
considering the season, she said laughingly that I must have
been surprised or astonished at her strange appearance of dress,
in black, on the verandah the last day I was up there. But it was
so comfortable she liked to wear it out there. I immediately
blundered by saying that I had been regarding it as a type of the
darkness of materiality which she was contending with. She at
once turned her head away, walking to a window, and showed
signs of being painfully affected to tears. I at once said I ought
not to have referred to that at this time. I looked at the Dr.; he
was looking a little sober; but in a minute Mrs. Eddy returned
to us and becoming seated, began to refer to the beauty of the
scenery about there, and her description of it led to reference to
peculiar appearances of it at remembered times, also, to how
she came to become possessed of this particular place, and most
of what she said, and I do not know but all, seemed, by the

occasional word or phrase, to have an underlying spiritual meaning. But she seemed so much like a little child in it all that I found difficulty in realizing that I was in the presence of the noted personage who had become so much to me in my life.

I asked her a question when she had been saying that she loved *nature* in people as well as in scenery. I asked if it was not a law of Being, or nature, that we should advance by impulses like the waves of the sea; or, like the ebbing and flowing of the tides? She said, that was the way while in our mortal thought, but that in the immortal Life it was all flowing, and no ebbing. "It is just action, action, action, always."

After fifteen or twenty minutes, when it seemed appropriate, she showed signs of closing the interview. She began to say, "I am busy" and then she broke in by saying, "Oh, I want Mr. Gilman to see the view from my upper verandah," signifying to the Dr. to go ahead and prepare the way for me to gain the full impressiveness of the view, at once, by opening some guards against the wind and cold of winter at the ends of the verandah. I was hesitating about going up the stairs first, before her but she says, "Oh, yes. You go right up," and she came directly after me. When we arrived most to the door opening on to the verandah, she said pleasantly and expectantly, "Wait a little until he gets the wind guards open so you will get the whole extent of the view at once." And then she led the way to her bedroom, just to the left, and pointed me out her bed where the sunlight shone, she said, "the very first thing in the morning." Then she took me in the room in the tower, which has windows looking out five ways from the northeast to the west, which is her room, as it is called. She showed me everything with the pleasure of a child. Then, when we went out on the verandah, while I was out looking at the points of interest the Dr. was showing me, Mrs. Eddy disappeared into the house. Then, pretty soon, she came out again with the identical black garb, or strange costume, on that she had on when I saw her that day, and she looked out with a significant arch smile as much as to say, even as she did say in substance, "You see, it is perfectly harmless, even if it *is* black and grotesque looking." After a little while, I was looking at some pictures in her room with the Dr., she having previously taken part in it, she went out, leaving me with the Dr. Taking off the black quaker bonnet, returning soon, she came up to me and bade me good-bye, offering her hand and said, "Come again."

While I was downstairs before coming up, after I had been referring a little to my motives or desires in the way of getting into practice in Christian Science, she said, "Trust in the Lord with thy whole heart and lean not to thine own understanding. In all thy ways acknowledge him and he shall direct thy paths" (Prov. III:5–6).

Her childlikeness impressed me the most, while the magnetic sense of personal presence is so little that it scarcely seemed I was in the presence of any one who could even really understand *Science and Health* much less one who could write it. This state of things I have been studying on all the day since, and this evening I just begin to see that the impressive magnetic sense of presence is not to be looked for in one of high attainments in Christian Science, but just the opposite.

The above is hastily and imperfectly written. If I could give it the time I could condense it one third and make it more readable but I trust you to make allowances for that. I thought you would be interested in these details.

Truly your friend,
James F. G.

I wish you a merry Christmas and a happy New Year.

— ✶ —

Concord, N.H.
Jan. 6, 1893

Dear Brother and Sister Clark[8]

Having had two interviews with Mrs. Eddy, I thought perhaps you would like to hear how she impressed me, and as they asked after you and sent their regards when I should write, I thought I may as well do so now.

I have been making a series of pictures of the new home named, "Pleasant View" for Mr. Bowers, a photographer here who is a particular friend of Mrs. Eddy. He is the one who has made a number of negatives of Mrs. Eddy within a year or two,

the photographs from which are ordered from all parts of the country. He has employed me in getting up these pictures of the new home and [says he intends to] give them appropriately grouped in one large frame, as a present to Mrs. Eddy. I suppose he expects to sell the photographs from the pictures to such as desire them, and doubtless many will want them.

The pictures I have just finished, the last ones this week. The two principal ones of the front and rear views were finished last week and were taken up there by Mr. Bowers for Mrs. Eddy to see. He reported to me that she was delighted with them, as indeed they [the rest of the household] all were. The next day she sent invitation to Mr. Bowers and to myself to take tea[9] with her New Year's, Sunday, evening which of course we accepted, and we were there from 5:30 until 8 o'clock.

Mr. Bowers is not yet a Christian Scientist by profession at least, but he has a lively appreciation for Mrs. Eddy. He has seen much of the world, has been in Europe, and traveled in India. He hates the churches generally, and has led, according to his own story, a dissolute life and is here [in Concord] to

"Pleasant View from the South"

"Pleasant View" as seen on the road from Concord

In this magnification from the previous view, the figures could represent Mrs. Eddy about to enter the carriage with Laura Sargent on the porch, Calvin Frye at the reins, and perhaps E. J. Foster Eddy at the horses' heads.

keep away from the allurements of city life as the only way for him to avoid the distruction incident there to. He is well educated and a person of much breadth of mind and talent and it is said Mrs. Eddy likes him because he is willing to pass for just what he is, neither more nor less and isn't in the least afraid of incurring her displeasure seemingly recognizing nothing but good intentions on her part, to be expressed in her own way whether by praise or rebuke, hence he goes right to the house whenever he wants to talk with her on any subject, or business or otherwise. I think this is mainly because he has no conception of the Science and sees her merely and mainly as a woman of the world. He assists Mrs. Eddy in her business transactions connected with improving the place in which he says he has saved her at least three or four thousand dollars for which he will take nothing. He is just proud to do anything for her that she wants him to do. He told her on New Year's to tell him what she wanted him to do and he would obey. Said he would like to study the Science under her instruction to which she said that she did not know that she should ever have another primary class she had so much else to attend to.

I have said that I had had two interviews. The first was Dec. 20th when the Dr. was there. I wrote out a description of this directly after, which perhaps I will send you, and you can return it to me when you have read it. I might want it at a future time.

On New Year's Mr. Bowers was with me and he is quite a talker so that the discourse was perhaps mainly between he and Mrs. Eddy although much of what she said was directed toward me—that is she then looked at me, or perhaps *through* me as it seemed. This time she appeared very much larger [in stature] to me than at the first time I met her. During the supper she did not want to eat much. It seemed mean to be eating, or rather to be gratifying my material cravings while she was talking in her expressive way of spiritual things.

After supper was over, conversation having taken a turn toward the logic of Science, she said: "Well, let us go into the parlor and there we will have a fine talk on Christian Science. I never tire of talking on that subject," to which place we went. And here she began to explain Christian Science, mainly to Mr. Bowers, beginning by explaining what God is, and then what the real man is as God's idea, and then what the material man claims to be, and from this, the letter of the Science, on to the more spiritual sense of it in which, more and more was reflected the Divine Beauty in which each of us felt how paltry were the purposes of material motives and aims. When the richness of the Love of Eternal Goodness might be ours to know, and realize always, if we would but become completely subject to it in the absolute self-surrender that this Love naturally involves.

The talk seemed just rounded up to its climax when the hack was announced at the door, having arrived at the time Mr. Bowers had appointed for it to come when we rode up from town. It scarcely seemed that we had been talking a half-hour instead of an hour and half.[10]

Mr. Bowers is quite material in his thought and has little natural perception of the Christian Science thought so she endeavored to make it very simple so that he would be able to see. Very little that she said to us this time was of that type that seemed to contain a deeper spiritual meaning than was apparent at first.

At the supper table Mr. Bowers said to her, Mrs. Eddy, "Christian Scientists call *Science and Health* a kind of revelation from God, but I think you originated that from your own superior mind and talent," to which she replied: "Oh, dear, no. I could not originate such a book. Why I have to study it myself in order to understand it. When I came to the writing each day, I did not know what I should write until my pen was dipped in the ink and I was ready to begin."

She said to me in the evening, "You must study the Science with me, Mr. Gilman." This was after I had been asking some question and she had briefly answered it.

Well, there is more that might be written than there is time or space to write. Since I have seen and talked with [Mrs. Eddy], I have a much different idea of her than I used to picture in my mind. Still I can see at times the look of one of the first photographs of her that I [obtained in Boston in 1886]. A few days after New Year's she sent me a gift of a copy of *Retrospection and Introspection* with my name written on the fly leaf under which was written "Respects of Author Mary B. G. Eddy 1892."

[It comes to me from] Mrs. Otis, after I was [at Mrs. Eddy's] the first time that [Mrs. Eddy said to Mrs. Otis that] she felt very easy and free in my company, or presence.

The last thing at the closing of the New Year's—"Love feast"—I guess I shall have to call it—she came very close to me and, taking my hand for the good-bye, she said in a loving, confidential way, that the picture I had made of the house and place, "was a complete expression of her ideal of what such a picture might be—a typical representation of the picture she had in mind of home."

During the talk in the latter part of the interview, she said, when reference had been made to the tendency of people to worship her personally, that she had had to work over her son, the Dr., for three years to get him corrected from loving her as a person to loving her as *God's idea.*

I have a couple of pictures of her which Mr. Bowers has made which I think I will mail to you. They lack in expression of course and I do not think they are as nicely made in some respects as they might be, particularly the hair, but they look more like her than the one I made the large one from. I think I may as well send you that also, as I do not want to use it as a specimen. They have one at the home—Pleasant View—from that same photo, also others from other photographs.

The pictures I have made of the place are no money to me above my expenses while doing the work, because I could not, and would not, limit the execution to the amount Mr. Bowers had in mind at first to pay. I felt it was best to make just the best picture that my ideality could aid me in doing without taking liberties with nature, and I think I succeeded pretty well. But if I have received little in money I have received richly what is worth far more—infinitely more—even of the things which money claims to be able to procure for us namely freedom from the sense of material bondage begotten seemingly from the sense of limited means. Mrs. Eddy reflects the Love and Truth of Perfect Goodness in such a way that it becomes plain that that Love of Goodness, and Goodness of Love is the only thing worth living for. The sense of it gives us freedom from all lesser interests and makes us know that it is completely within the reach of each of us when we are ready with self-surrender for its sake....."The Way in the flesh is the suffering that leads out of the flesh,"[11] says Mrs. Eddy in "Unity of Good."

I will send you photos from my drawings when Mr. Bowers gets some made which will be soon.

Mary Baker Eddy
Conté crayon drawing by James F. Gilman,
after an 1886 photograph by H. G. Smith

The meetings at Mrs. Otis' room I find to be very profitable.... If I talk a high line of Science to her she will likely say, "Oh, yes, that is the *theory* and all right if you can live up to it, but we have to learn to walk before we can fly." If her students are slow to try to do anything because they think they do not know enough, she will talk just the other way. But generally she is much given to talking that we are very small indeed in Science as yet. That the oldest students are scarcely more than twelve years of age, and most of them are under five or six, that, in fact, there is but one Scientist in the world who justifies that name— Mrs. Eddy. When I was at Mrs. Eddy's New Year's evening my own supposed attainments seemed very small indeed, mere husks without corn.... Mrs. Eddy herself says that she is very little in the sight of God, and has done but a very little, particularly when the infinite spiritual blessings which God's Love has bestowed, and is bestowing daily, are considered. To go down in our own estimation is to go up in God's is according to Christian Science. This of course is not new: I have heard you advocate the same and have seen you demonstrate it. But we do not ever I suppose realize this lowliness except when the Love and Truth of God is a living fire in our consciousness, then the lowliness is natural and spontaneous, sweet....

Give my respects to Mr. Bates and his family. I suppose, as usual, they attend your sunday meetings. Does the interest appear to be growing a little? We cannot expect much. The attendance here is from fifteen to thirty, but Concord is about three times as large in population as Barre, and the practitioner here gives her whole time to the work. Well, good-bye and best wishes. You will have to begin this in the morning to get it read the same day it is so long.

Jan. 15

Since writing the major part of the above, I have been to
Mrs. Eddy's again, this time in answer to her invitation by let-
ter to come to her house at 7 o'clock Thursday evening (Jan. 12)
and she would talk with me. This was prompted by my letter of
acknowledgment of the gift of *Retrospection and Introspection* in
which I seemed to be holding error in my thought in some
forms which she wished to correct. It was a very pleasant talk
indeed, and she did not once directly refer to what I had writ-
ten in my letter, but I have found since that the error spoken of
has faded so far as a clearer consciousness of God's Goodness
makes me to judge. Among many other things that she told me
was this: that she was going to have a Normal class of advanced
students, not necessarily old ones (she did not use these words),
but those advanced in spiritual growth and perception—she
was going to have the class when God's time came, for she says,
"I always wait for that now." "Those who enter this class must
have on *'the wedding garment'* else there will be no fitness, or
value, in their entering the class. I used to teach nearly all who
came—that was my work then. *Now* my privilege and duty is
to *select*."

Those who spontaneously and unconsciously reveal that they
love the spiritual *realization* of Divine Love and Truth *more*
than they love any thing else I judge to be the ones whom she
credits with having on the wedding garment. I judge this more
by the thought which she reflects than by any definite state-
ment which she makes. In her talk she makes very few direct
definite statements, but rather *suggests* to your thought. This is
a way of teaching that I like so much. This general way of
reflecting the Truth and Love of God is perfectly calculated to

inspire the student with the idea of God which he is adapted to know and realize at that time, and in such a way that he has the valuable sense of its originality. This begets the assurance that is needed to support his further advancement. The talk lasted an hour and a half.... All my sense of bondage on account of poverty and indebtedness has gone because I see that when we have the sense of God's Love, we then have *everything*. It appears clear that it has been the faithful purpose of this Love that I shall not be left to the error of *seeming* to gain freedom from bondage by becoming possessed of the material means that would *seem* to do it, and which claims to be able to do it, when the Truth is that Love's freedom is the *only* freedom, which when truly realized will soon become outwardly manifest in due time.

J. F. G.

There is one great encouragement "Wedding garments" are not beyond the reach of any who earnestly desire them and live for their possession.

— * —

Concord, N.H.
Jan. 17, 1893

Dear Friend Carrie.

Your welcome letter was received last evening. I see by the receiving postmark that it arrived at the Office here on Jan. 2. I engaged a box the first of January since which I have not called for my mail at the general delivery supposing that if there was any they would put it in the box. It is evident there must be a laxity of discipline in this Office as I have had trouble to get my mail ever since I came here. I shall follow them up pretty close now. This of yours was put into my box yesterday with another from Boston that came Sunday. Seeing how long yours had been here I enquired at the general delivery this morning and found four more letters or cards, two of which had been there over a week, and yet they occasionally got some mail into my box which was what misled me into supposing that consequently they got it all in.

I don't have it delivered because they only deliver what is marked with my street and number, and as this necessitates my going to the Office every day and enquiring for mail that would not be marked that way, I concluded it best to get it all there. Where one doesn't know that they shall remain in a place three days or a week, St. and No. are not in order.—There that is enough of that I guess—isn't it? The mail will be all right in future.

Well, I have a good deal of thought to send you but just at present it is in Barre, Vt. on a visit: that is, much that I have desired to express to you I have just written out and sent to Mr. Clark with the request that he return it in a few days so that I can send to you without rewriting it. You see I try to write it all and it takes me much time to do it. I must begin to write shorter letters.

I will however write a little in this and send it along so that you may know that I have received yours.

When I got the two larger, and principal, pictures done of Mrs. Eddy's place, Mr. Bowers, being much pleased with them took them up to show to Mrs. Eddy. He reported that she was delighted with them. It was the Thursday before New Year's. Friday, Mr. Bowers and I received an invitation from Mrs. Eddy to take tea with her on New Year's (Sunday) evening, and we were there from half past five until 8 o'clock.

I will not attempt here to redescribe it but will send you what I have sent to Mr. Clark when he returns it. I will say briefly however, that we spent a very pleasant and profitable evening.

Mrs. Eddy talked freely on the subject of Christian Science to us, particularly to Mr. Bowers, who understands but little of it; and does not accept of it, but admires Mrs. Eddy. She tried to make [it] simple, so that he could receive it. As she talked, she gradually impressed us more and more with the sense of the divine beauty of Love, so that it became perfectly plain to our understanding that that glorious state of mind included all goodness, all reality, being perfectly satisfying, making lesser possessions, aims, or desires appear paltry and poor, indeed.

Three days later she sent me *Retrospection and Introspection* with my name written on the flyleaf in her own hand writing with, "Respects of Author, Mary B. G. Eddy, 1892" under it. I acknowledged it in a short letter. In two or three days she wrote me a letter saying:

[Tues. Eve Jan. 9, 1893]
Your letter interests me. You seem standing in awe of Good, and doubting your own reflection of it, but seeing the false assume the reflex shadow, you mentally sketch it as your self *but it is not.* Call on me Thurs. eve. at 7 o'clock, and I will talk with you again.
Very Respectfully,
Mary B. G. Eddy

Of course I accepted, and she gave me a very pleasant and valuable talk, lasting from 7 until 8:30 o'clock. In the waiting room, or library it was, that there she came in and sat down with

me alone, and told me so much; and delicate things concerning
her own history, and experience in such a simple, unassuming
way that I forgot *almost* that she was an important personage,
and that I was enjoying a very rare privilege. She moved me
greatly by saying that she wanted I should receive instruction
under her in the selected Normal class she expected to teach, she
could not tell just when, but when God's time came. She says,
"I always wait for that, now." She said, "I used to teach nearly
everybody who applied. It was right I should then, but now
God's way is that I may select such as are found prepared to
receive the advanced instruction. In the olden times, you know,
they invited guests to the wedding feast but if one came not hav-
ing on the wedding garment he could not participate with the
rest, and that is the way it must be in this instruction."

She said this in a childlike, pleasant way that screened its
importance for the time, but afterwards, when the memory of
what she has said agitates, and turns, and overturns the thought,
the import of it grows upon the sense, until if one is in earnest,
they know that unless they so *strive* to gain the constant sense of
God's Love and Truth so that it is seen to be worth more than
all else that seems to be, but is not, they will be found without
the needed wedding garment, hence will be debarred from what
might have been an open way to go higher, had there been readi-
ness for it. I think she is taking this way to spur students to more
spiritual living. I feel that I am unprepared now; I find that my
thought and understanding has been little enough. To say it is
receiving many corrections is inadequate to express it fully.

I think you have been growing wonderfully during the past
six months. I believe you are ready to enter this class Mrs. Eddy
speaks of and perhaps you will. She told me she did not think

about the tuition in this class. I suppose she, knowing my limited means, wanted I should see that the lack of money could not close the door against me. I cannot think that she really thinks I am much advanced, or that what she says is to be regarded as equivalent to having been selected. I will say that she told Mrs. Otis, the practitioner here, that she felt very easy in my presence. I believe I have already written this in Mr. Clark's letter, which you will get later. The thought reflected to me in this last interview I believe has broken the sense of bondage connected with lack of material means. It is clear that nothing is worth living for but this sense of Love and Truth. Money will not procure this; the lack of it cannot bar it from me or from anyone. "More we do not want; more we do not need; more we cannot have."

A valuable thought to me just now is that error silently accumulates in the *unconscious* thought, and we need the cleansing often that Truth affords *not waiting until it becomes apparent* to the *conscious* thought before we apply the cleansing remedy. It is better to keep well, than it is to allow ourselves to get sick and be doctored. A man that is always having fits of sickness is not to be depended upon.

You have kindly remembered me with a very pretty calendar arrangement for which please accept my sincere thanks. Whenever I look where it hangs in my room I shall think of a very dear friend whom I long have known, in whose spiritual progress I greatly rejoice as well as profit by.

I will perhaps be able to send you some photographic copies from the pictures I have been making by the first of next week. I never was engaged on a picture in which fresh and good thoughts came so easily and rapidly as on this one. It was a work of love to do it. And I never have expected to feel so rewarded for the application I have given to gain mastery in art-work as I have felt in this. Mr. Bowers says he is going to take it to the World's Fair at Chicago.[12] What Mrs. Eddy said to me of it is in the letters I have sent to Mr. Clark, which I think you will get in a week or two.

Yours very truly,
James F. Gilman

— ✳ —

Boston, Mass.
Jan. 27, 1893

My dear friend Carrie.

You see by the heading of this that I am in Boston. I am a student in Dr. Foster Eddy's class that he is now holding very quietly, and without public announcement. No students, or rather, Scientists here, know of it except those connected with the Journal Office. This is to guard against the adverse influence—in belief—of the opposition here, I am told. There are 23 in the class, and they are composed of such as have already studied (in the main) with students of Mrs. Eddy, but who desire, doubtless, to become eligible to study in Mrs. Eddy's advanced normal class, when she has it, as well as to gain the advantage of the advanced understanding which the Dr., being so near Mrs. Eddy, is naturally supposed to be in possession of.

Last evening was the second lecture, of which there are to be seven in all, given on seven successive evenings.... I have referred to the teaching as being lectures, but they are not so in the ordinary sense, but his way is to ask questions. He will ask the same question clear around the class getting the thought of each stirring to elicit from the student the thought he wishes to impart and impress. He seems careful that some leading impressive, important thought shall be left on the student's mind each lesson, or lecture.

Well, you see I am getting on pretty well. The Dr. was up to Concord on Sunday last and went back to Boston on Monday. He left word with Mrs. Otis that he was to hold this class and that I might become a member if I desired and he would take the tuition in my work when I could give it. I saw the Dr. yesterday at 62 Boylston St. for two or three minutes and among other things he said that, "Mother said to me on Sunday that she would like me to take you through my class, so that you could be one of her normal class when she held it." The idea she has given out, as you know, is that only those who have been her primary students, or the Dr.'s primary students, can come into that class—that is one qualification.

The day before I came here she wrote me a letter in answer to one I had addressed to her a week or ten days before, just after the talk she gave me that Thursday evening. The letter is as follows:

[Jan 23, 1893]

My dear friend.

Your last letter gave me a sweet sense of your character. I have done as you requested, written Mr. Bowers that you declined to accept the share in copyright.

I ask a favor of you, viz. keep me informed of your P.O. address in some way easy for yourself, a letter from you would be valued but this may be asking too much at each change of place.

I want you to paint a portrait of me, just such an one as I will describe, of other days, or one at this advanced age. I have not decided which. I shall have this done

when I get time and *you can do it.* But I may never get
the time, for "my times are in His hands." I want to
employ it all in His service and to bless the race.

Most Truly,
Mary B. G. Eddy

Now, my dear friend, what do you think of that? The thought
has lately entered my mind in a harmonious way that I would
like the way to open for me to engage my best effort to make a
portrait of her that would do justice to the greatness and spiritual
quality of the subject: a portrait that would be valued greatly by
all lovers and followers of the Truth as it shines in Christian
Science. I *have* thought that I could not do it, and *now* I feel it
more or less; but the inspiring quality of her thought suggests
beautiful designs, in a vague way as yet, that promise well for suc-
cess. It is a religious work to do it well, and such a picture is what
is wanted, sincerely and widely. She emphasizes *"you can do it"*
which ought to be sufficient inspiration....

Yours very truly,
James F. Gilman

— * —

To Carrie Huse

Concord, N.H.
Feb. 19, 1893

My dear Friend.

Yours is duly received, and I find it very welcome and interesting,
& spiritual and upbuilding in its Christian character as all your let-
ters have been rapidly growing to be.

If I were to undertake to write all that is new and interesting in my experience here, I should have a great task on my hands. I have glad news to write; and, I supposed from last Sunday eve until Thursday eve that I had also sad news to refer to. But a letter from Mrs. Eddy received then has modified much of the sad characters of it, while the glad news referred to is just as glad.

The situation is this, that Mrs. Eddy was in anguish last Sunday evening [Feb. 12], at which time I was there in response to her invitation, because of the evidences of dishonor which it appeared was being brought upon the Cause by her son, Dr. Foster Eddy, by his course in connection with teaching a class of students without her knowledge or consent (granting them C.S.B. degrees without the authority to do so, and granting them admission, so far as he could do so, to the Parent C.S. Association in Boston). The evidences were mainly elicited from me, in response to questions she asked me, the import of which I did not then know. It was not apparently so much that he had ventured to teach without consulting her, but partly that he had not grown to a fitness to teach and partly other serious considerations. She had been watching and waiting, she said, for him to grow to that fitness, but had seen very recently that he had not attained to it yet, and my innocent answers to her questions confirmed this view more than even she had expected, apparently.

I cannot undertake to literally describe the varying manifestations of intense feeling. It would be sacrilege; but in it I *saw the real Mrs. Eddy*, not fully at that time, but more fully two or three days afterwards. I trust I may never forget that vision of the Holy, Loved One of God. It made me feel that I had but one purpose in life, and that to labor to bring this realization of the Beloved—the Real One to the understanding of men in every quarter of the earth. I asked her if there was something I could do to relieve her of some of the burden she felt. Immediately she answered: "Yes, three times daily seek consecration to Christ's work," which I promised I would do. There is but one *Real One,* and it is the vision of that One as my Life, and your Life, and Mrs. Eddy's Life, and *everyone's* Life, really, that I refer to above as the "Holy, Loved One of God."

I suggested that I might write a letter to the Dr. that might do good, to which she assented more or less absently, but later she thought perhaps I better not, as it might only stir ill feeling. Tuesday I thought perhaps I could do good by writing such a letter, so I wrote it, directing it to the Dr. in Boston, leaving it unsealed, and putting it into another, and larger envelope, and sealing that, sent it to Mrs. Eddy, asking her to read and, if it seemed well, to seal up and post it. The letter did not refer to having had any interview with his mother, but called him to sharp account in a way that accorded with his instructions in the class, that we should faithfully do if we found another to be in the wrong. Well, there was a good deal of manifest love in the letter, notwithstanding a spade was called a spade. Thursday evening I received a letter from Mrs. E. as follows:

> My very dear Friend,
>   Your letter strikes home—but with Christian intent, and I believe will do my son good. Oh! what a spirit of love impelled it! This is Christian kindness, brotherly love. I thank you my brother. May

God bless your purpose. My son was here since you
were. He had an *excuse* which I will name to you.
Call on me next Sunday evening.

> With gratitude,
> Mother

I had addressed her as, "Dear Mother in Truth" in the note
accompanying the Dr.'s letter, as I felt particularly justified in
doing after the events of Sunday evening. You see, the solicitude
she manifested for my spiritual welfare, seeing as she did, that I
had grown material in my thought since last she had seen me,
and I directly from the class, was *so eloquent.*

I had been up there the evening before this, that being the
evening she had designated when she asked me first to come;
but she found me so material that she sent me home after fif-
teen minutes or so, giving me a copy of *Pond and Purpose*[13] ask-
ing me to study it and come up the following evening, as she
had had company that day and there were things that needed
her attention.

Sunday evening, after a trifle of hesitation, she proceeded to
her apparently painful task, I suspecting nothing, not realizing
the glamour that had come over my thought, thinking of great
pictures I was to make of a great subject with the *material*
means that would be afforded to deliver me from the evil &c.
of poverty, and limitations as of old. Her first words after we
had become seated (she directly across the centre table from
me), were in reference to the limitations of her time. I said, after
a little pause, "Perhaps there is nothing to be said that need take
your time tonight."

(I was thinking of pictures, and thought unexpected duties

might be calling for her time, which I could wait for.) She immediately answered: "Yes, there is." She then asked with anxious solicitude in which there was a tender reproachfulness, "Mr. Gilman, *do you feel an added sense of consecration since you have been through the class?* (Mrs. Sargent[14] who helps her and who had been to the Association[15] meeting in Boston and there learned for the first time that the Dr. had been holding a class, had told Mrs. E. of this class. Mrs. E. had referred to it briefly the night before to me, saying then in a somewhat strained manner, "So you have been through a class.") "Now," she said, "tell me, Mr. Gilman, just *simply* and *truly* as it honestly appears to you." There was such a childlike simplicity and earnest purity about this that until we have been questioned that way we can have no idea of the thoughts of spiritual goodness it suggested or reflected.

I answered truly that I did not, but began to try to account for it on the ground that I felt consecrated before, hence there would naturally be less sense of its increase. In this it began to dawn upon me that she was not approving of the class being held by the Dr., and my thought was at once to screen the Dr., both to save him from censure and Mrs. Eddy from pain, and also it seemed mean to go back on the absent Dr. But Mrs. Eddy began to say, as soon as I began to talk to praise the Dr. (I wanted to praise what I really could and keep silent on what I did not like very well), that I wasn't talking frankly. "Now," she said, tenderly pleading, *"just be Mr. Gilman, just as you were when I first saw you.* Oh! this subtle glamour of animal magnetism![16] You seemed so free from it then!"

I then told her that the Dr. seemed to rise, every evening, in spiritual impressiveness until after the fourth; the following three evenings seemed to be lacking; the last one seeming to have nothing to it, to speak of, and that in this I had felt a disappointment.

"Now," she said, "Mr. *Gilman* is talking. Of course the spiritual impressiveness should have continued to the last, when it should have been the most so. Oh!" she said, "How dreadful this is!" and she began to walk the floor a little, asking me if I did not think it would be better if no teaching *whatever* were done; but just let people become instructed through *Science and Health*.[17] I answered in the affirmative then, because it was in the line of former consideration of the matter somewhat. But tonight I go up again and I shall modify that thought, if I think of it, which however, will not make much difference with her, probably.

I cannot attempt to describe what followed during over an hour. I tried to comfort her by telling her that it would all result in greater glory to the Cause and to God as we should see later. "Yes" she said despairingly, "God makes the wrath of man to praise Him." She said, "It isn't the personal feeling that agitates me; it is the effect of it upon the Cause. Personally, I could take the dear boy to my arms and forget it all." First it was questions to me; then it was righteous indignation expressed as the answers seemed to call for it; then it was explanation of the right thought. Then despairing thought found utterance—until it was found to be 8:30 o'clock when I took my leave, promising that I would carry out faithfully her directions of seeking frequent consecration to Christlike work. May I ever faithfully keep it, is my earnest desire.

Monday P.M.
Feb. 20

We're having a terrible blizzard today. Everything blocked in a business way. I went to Mrs. Eddy's last eve and found her in a completely resigned and serene state of mind. She began talking at once of spiritual things, about trusting completely in the Lord. If things go well, then we may trust in the Lord and be thankful. If they seem to go ill, then we may still trust in the Lord, and wait for the correcting power of His Right Arm, and be thankful that we may get beneath the shadow of His wings. If things seem to be at a standstill and we cannot tell what to do, we can wait then and rest, and in this be thankful, but always to enter into His courts with Thanksgiving. Says she to me," 'Commit thy way unto the Lord; trust also in him; and he shall bring it to pass.' You see," said she, "it is not enough that we commit our way unto Him, but to *trust also.* 'And he shall bring forth thy righteousness as the light; and thy judgment as the noonday.' (Psalms xxxvii 5, 6.) There you see," said she with such a joyous face and look of resignation, "just how it will be."

Then she went on to describe in detail her experience in Chicago, when she addressed such a large audience there (4,000 or more)[18] and how she knew nothing of the address until the moment she was expected to go on to the stage to begin the address. She then related that she consented to be there at that convention on the understanding that she was not to be expected to address them, but that she was to be one with them, with the privilege of saying a word at any time if it seemed best, just as any one of them would. After she had been there a little, she inquired for one of their programes, but did not get hold of one from various reasons.

She came in on the morning of the address with others, finding the great Hall completely packed, and it was then that she learned for the first time that she was down on the programe to address them and they were waiting for her to go on to the stage then. She said her heart sank within her. "I turned around and said to Scientists with me: 'This is downright dishonesty. I never can carry this out. I haven't even thought of a subject.' Mrs. Sargent was with me and she looked at me courageously and said, 'God will put words into your mouth to speak, I am sure.'" Mrs. E. paused here to say, "Mrs. Sargent has been with me in more trying times than any other woman," and she repeated the thought that she was a true and helpful friend. (Mrs. Sargent assists Mrs. E. and always receives me at the door, and welcomes me to the sitting-room, and takes my coat and hat. She is very winsome and spiritual, I think.)

"Well," said Mrs. Eddy, "God's leading seemed to be more toward the stage than away, so I went thinking there would be some provision." Then she explained how it happened that she had been put on the programe without her knowledge. "Well, when I got on to the platform, every one of that vast audience arose as one man, spontaneously, and unexpectedly to the audience even. It was said there then no one had ever known of such a thing before. When I got on to the stage, the thought of my subject came to my mind—'Science and the Senses.'[19] It was almost just what I had dreamed a short time previously; I could not tell exactly when, nor just about the dream. Then the audience sang, 'Nearer my God to Thee,' and I felt full of the Spirit and I was just ready; my fear had all left me, you see; and I talked to them for an hour, and then I said I should weary them, but they called out for me to 'go on' and I talked a half hour more. Then when I got through, there was a great rush toward the stage, and the detectives and policemen were about to open a way out, but there were a lot of people down in front holding up their hands and being held up by others, and call-'ing upon me to help them, and I said to the police, or those in charge, '*Wait,* there is work here yet to do,' and I received acknowledgments from many afterward, saying they had been entirely healed of their diseases, one a so-called hopeless case of diabetes and others too numerous to mention. Then the police cleared the way for my hack where an immense crowd were striving to see me (it was a morning session, hence it was daylight) and, at the hotel the crowd filled the corridors and even the elevator, until I could get to my room where I was free once again. I tell you this," she said, "because in this you may see that if we trust in the Lord, He will uphold us."

Then she began to refer to the Dr.'s excuse, and said he had been governed by a precedent which she had unwittingly established near the time she had closed her College when in a last normal class she had received his students (nearly all of the Dr.'s class had studied already and therefore were not eligible as primary students to Dr. Eddy's class as she had intended it, hence his offense). "It was not a good excuse, but it was enough to let me know that as a choice of two evils, it was better that it remain than to try to correct it now. I hope the dear ones will all do well," said she kindly and cheerfully and hopefully.

This was about all she said concerning the Dr., but some

word turned the conversation toward the good I had received in consequence of her solicitude for me. I told her, love like hers never could be repaid. She leaned forward and raised herself toward me in her chair and said, with much emphasis and feeling, "You have repaid me already tonight. You are yourself again. To do such work is what I live for."

I saw what she meant and told her that as I carried into practice the effort at consecration, I gained a clear view of the magnetism that had been dominating me, and the vast and distinct difference between it and the sense of the Real One, the Christ, which I had been led to behold through her reflection of it the Sunday eve before; and that I hoped that the future would show that her kindness and love was not in vain. I had, I felt, seen the *Real* Mrs. Eddy.

"Yes," she said, "You will be able through God's strength to do the work you desire to." She soon closed, saying her minutes were precious. I had been there about a half hour.

One other remark I meant to have added to my last but one. She said: "When you were here that Saturday night, I could see you were just taken up and carried away by the animal magnetism, so that you were completely self-satisfied and pleased, all about—*nothing.*" She paused after this a little and then added, *"nothing"* in a happy, smiling way that could give nobody offense.

You have asked me if she looks like her photographs? A *little* like one or two of them after you have seen her awhile. I can see the looks of the youngest one of the two I got in Boston in '86 the most of any except that her hair is an iron gray, almost white, and yet not white by a considerable. Her hair is abundant and it looks very pretty the way she wears it. The late picture which you have seen that Mr. Bowers makes looks to me as she does some times, but it looks larger than she does, and not expressive. Mr. Bowers has promised to get out some small photographs soon of the picture I have made of the place, but he has been driven with work so that this has been delayed. He is going to send the picture to N. York to have some large photogravure made as soon as he gets his copyright papers.

You write that you think I have earned the privileges I am now accorded. That is not so. In the truer view I get sometimes of myself that is just where I am lacking. There is a looseness in my makeup in some way by which the sterling, reliable character seems to be lacking so that I find myself distrustful of the future. Of course spiritually and scientifically I know this is not so. I have lived for my own glory, and ease, and whims so much that to stand for duty only is a task I am not strong and rigorous in at all. May the truth keep me from presumptuousness in thought. More meekness I must have or I shall be lost....

You must keep confidentially what I have written concerning the Dr. and Mrs. Eddy in the last interviews. I need not to write this for you are doubly prudent on such matters.

Well Good-bye

Truly your friend with love,

James F. Gilman

There is one thing more I would like to write. When I am at Mrs. Eddy's, in her presence I find myself in a consciousness that is a mixture of pleasure and pain, of a mentally material nature, and in this I feel not satisfaction or real ease. Neither, while there do I gain spiritual realization in the deep and true sense; but afterwards Mrs. Eddy's words and thoughts agitate my thought, until finally they bring me the spiritual sense I rejoice in. I feel so exposed to her thought while I am there that I feel selfish all through as soon as I begin to speak; and equally so if I do not; because then stupidity seems to rule me. Doubtless it is the rebuke of her spirituality that I feel. I will add that there was one exception to this in a considerable degree and that was the Saturday evening when she found me so material that I was mostly insensible to even this rebuking sense of Spirit. It took something as material as literal rebuke of mouth to startle and awaken me.

Mrs. Eddy has given me "Unity of Good" which I am very glad of as I think there is a wonderful amount of thought in that.

Truly

J. F. Gilman

I am making some pictures of horses here for people: have a crayon portrait to make, have made a watercolor painting of an old-fashioned farm place for a specimen of residence picture known to people here. I call it "Old New England." It is in winter time and there is a horse and sleigh in the road. The pictures of Mrs. Eddy's place were made in monochrome, water color— Ivory Black. They look like steel engraving a little away.

Truly   J. F. G.

One or two things more that Mrs. Eddy said, I will write. Some word or reference had been made to healing on the evening of a week ago, and she asked in the, as yet unquieted spell of indignation, "He taught you how to heal did he not?" I answered,

"Yes, but in a less definite way than I had expected." I asked him if it was necessary or important to know the name of the disease or what the claim of the disease was to be healed. And he said, "No, it was not. In fact the less you know about that the better. You just need to realize God's allness and that all forms of disease are nothing but illusion." *"What?"* she exclaimed interrogatively, in a deep alto voice (her usual voice is soprano). Then she exclaimed in the same key, *"You have not been taught!* Oh! Oh! Why, that is the way *I* heal, but students can't begin there anymore than art pupils can begin to make pictures before they make outlines." I appreciated that and said I should think that would be the way it would be. "Certainly," she said.

She said to me last night that I could heal, asked me if I had had any experience. I told her not, except my own case. I had been able to do that. "Well, that is a great deal; that is more than some Scientists can do who have good success with others." She meant to neutralize and soften a little, impressions she might have made in the intense expression she had used before.

She said to me last night that I might know when I was getting into the toils of animal magnetism by watching my thought to note when the self-satisfied, pleased-at-nothing (she did not use exactly these words, but words amounting to the same) thought, or consciousness, began to take the place of the humility and meekness and earnest desire for the spiritual things of God. "Ye cannot serve God and mammon. These two states of mind cannot dwell together."

She asked me a week ago to consider what had been talked between us as confidential, but I am sure in writing of it to you I violate no compact in that respect in the true spirit of it. I should not be afraid for her to see this letter or know of it. Of course you are the only one I write it, and to you not for the sake of telling news but for the suggestiveness of good it may bear and partly too because I wished to write it out while it is fresh in memory. A future reference to it may be of value and service.

Again I say Good-bye.

J. F. G.

MONDAY, FEBRUARY 20, 1893

Mrs. Eddy, a short time previous, told me when last I was there that I might know when I was getting into the snares of animal magnetism by watching the state of my thought if I found it to be of the self-satisfied order, egotistic, pleased with our progress generally—the pleased at nothing, self complacent kind, it might then be known that I was astray. But that when I found myself in a sense of meekness and humility, dissatisfied with personal sense and willing to do anything, and bear anything for the sake of the Christ realized, I might be sure I was in the way of health and holiness. These two states of mind never mingle—one is of earth, the other of heaven. This difference would appear in our unguarded, spontaneous moments when our true motives come to the surface and appear in our thoughts and acts unchallenged, rather than in our conscious professions.

FRIDAY, MARCH 3, 1893

Last evening at Pleasant View, we were speaking of Mr. Bowers, the photographer, who while much interested in

Mrs. Eddy, was yet not interested in the spiritual way of a Christian Scientist. I had told her he had asked me to go with him to see some good show theatricals then being acted in town, and I had declined; and he appeared to think perhaps I had some Christian Science scruples about going to a theater for entertainment, for he said to me, "It's all right for Christian Scientists to go to theatricals if they want to go, isn't it?" I replied, "It may be, if they want to go," but I had found out for me to do so was to get my mind filled with material thoughts opposed to the Christian Science I professed to be governed by, and that afterwards I had to work hard in the Christian Science way to mentally get them out of my thought again, which made the theatrical entertainment cost more than it came to, I thought.

After I said this to Mrs. Eddy, I felt it perhaps was not a very wise or Christian Science answer to one in Mr. Bowers's plane of thought, and so I said so to Mrs. Eddy. To this she replied quickly and with some emphasis, "You answered him rightly." I still felt in doubt as to whether Mrs. Eddy fully understood what I meant, and proceeded to say more definitely that while I could see the answer was true enough, I lacked tact or something else in giving it to one on Mr. Bowers's plane of thinking. To this Mrs. Eddy appeared to rise immediately to perceive the need and to improve the opportunity to rebuke an error of the human mind, for raising herself somewhat, she said with greater emphasis and decision, *"You answered him just right."* She did not, however, add one word to this as explanatory of the same. She left it then with God.

This unexpected repeated emphasis made a deep impression upon my mind. It appeared to me a sharp rebuke of something

I could not just know exactly what. It finally became clear to me that it was not on Mr. Bowers's account particularly that she had been impelled to give the second statement of the same thought such emphasis, but rather that I should see more decisively the rightness of my answer in a broad sense, because the most of mankind appear as engaged much of the time in getting filled with erroneous temporary entertainments, that afterwards they must work hard to get out of mind before they can go forward to their true sense of good. Our textbook says: "We soil our garments with conservatism, and afterwards we must wash them clean."[20]

Pleasant View.

CONCORD, N. H., March 8, 93

Mr. J. F. Gilman:

Mrs. Eddy says she has a matter of business in your line about which she would like to talk with you and asks when it would be convenient for you to call and see her. Please name the earliest date available.

Yours truly

C. A. Frye

"A matter of business in your line"

Illustrating *Christ and Christmas*

Pleasant View, Concord, N.H.
March 8, 1893

Mr. J. F. Gilman

Mrs. Eddy says she has a matter of business in your line about which she would like to talk with you and asks when it would be convenient for you to call and see her. Please name the earliest date available.

Yours truly,
C. A. Frye

Pleasant View, Concord
March 10, 1893

Mr. Gilman
Dear Sir

Mrs. Eddy finds that she cannot see you this pm and asks that you call tomorrow (Sat.) at 1 PM or 7 PM

Respectfully yours,
C. A. Frye

FRIDAY, MARCH 10, 1893

Went up to St. Paul's School, a wealthy, widely known
Episcopal educational institution three or four miles west of
Concord, with a letter of introduction and commendation
from Howard Hill, an Episcopal clergyman living in Concord,
N. H., but formerly of Montpelier, Vt., where I became favor-
ably known to him as an artist and maker of etchings.[1] I went
up in the hope of getting the school authorities there interested
in some form of picture work to represent the school buildings,
&c. I was not altogether successful because of the absence of the
president of the school. I was still in vicinity of the school
buildings, but walking homeward toward Concord somewhat
downcast because of my partial failure to get some art work to
do, when a carriage coming along behind overtook me. I being
on the side path, and the driver of the hack called out to me to
attract my attention, he having stopped the horses. He
motioned me to come near the carriage, and as I did so I saw it
was Mr. Frye, Mrs. Eddy's secretary, who said Mrs. Eddy would
like to speak with me, and going to the carriage door was
greeted by her with a smile of recognition. She said she would
like to have me call at her house the following evening at 7:30
o'clock, if I would as she had something she wished to talk with
me about.

I think I can never forget the beautiful picture impressed
upon my mind by this brief incident, the centre of interest of
which is in the pure light figure of Mrs. Eddy sitting in her car-
riage (of enclosed form to suit the season) as I first saw her at
the opening of the carriage door extending to me in her gentle
way her hand and a smiling face that appeared to me then

under the peculiar circumstances of the hour as an angel from heaven who had intervened just at the right moment needed to save me from the burden of seeking for work to do in order to live from people who would not have my work anyway if they knew I was favorably interested in Christian Science, and Mrs. Eddy. This was what the Rev. Mr. Hill had told me when he gave me the letter of commendation to the St. Paul's School authorities.

SATURDAY, MARCH 11, 1893

Went to Mrs. Eddy's this evening in fulfillment of her request at the St. Paul's School locality. She told me that she had written a poem which she had entitled *Christ and Christmas* and said she wanted to have some illustrations made for it, and asked me if I thought I could make them.

In reply to her question I said I should be very glad to undertake to make such illustrations if she had confidence in my ability to do it satisfactorily. She said she felt confident I could do anything in accord with my ideal aspirations as an artist. Mrs. Eddy then read me the poem which appeared to me very beautiful and grand. I told her I felt sure after I had had time to think it over that designs would begin to come to my thought that would lead up to what would prove to be desirable. She replied that she wanted that I should go on and see what designs would come to me when left entirely to myself and God. She said she would not at present make a single suggestion. Mrs. Eddy appeared to desire to leave the field of my thought entirely to what might be brought out by my obedience to Truth's revealings when left wholly to heeding the spiritual intuitions thereby awakened. "You can make sketches," she said, "and bring them for my inspection; then perhaps I shall have thoughts that will help to the clearer apprehension of what will be best."

Mrs. Eddy then gave me a copy of the poem telling me earnestly to *let no one know anything about this undertaking.* "Keep it sacredly to yourself," she said, "and look to God for guidance and inspiration."

WEDNESDAY, MARCH 15, 1893

Wrote as follows to Mrs. Eddy:

> My Dear Friend,
>
> I find your poem sublime and beautiful in its grand expression of Truth in simplicity and unity of idea and purpose. It is full of vital meaning in its terse presentment of the Christian Science Idea in a fresh original way. Its vital thought appears plainer as it is read many times as it needs to be. The "lone brave star" is Divine Science, the "seven-hued white" that is "Good." What earthly symbol can be imagined that can forcibly typify such an original symmetrical spiritual concept? My imagination that I have thought boundless cannot yet reach it and doubtless never can. Can yours, think you? The pencil cannot always follow the pen. I have had a number of conceptions that I think will serve as interpretations of other

branches of the one thought in the poem which I will go up and explain to you when you would like to hear of them or suggest of yours. The import of this work grows upon my thought and the sooner I can get down to the demonstration the better it will suit me. Would you like to see me Sat. evening a half hour or so? I will go up and if the evening finds you busy, or not yet ready, I shall find the walk up no hardship. I wish you always to feel free from any sense of bondage that I might inadvertently give rise to in our undertakings.

Yours very truly,
James F. Gilman

SATURDAY, MARCH 18, 1893

Went up to Pleasant View to talk with Mrs. Eddy about some conceptions of designs. Found her in grief because of the way some things appeared to be going in Boston.[2] At this interview she showed me an illustrated poem written by Phillips Brooks[3] which was beautifully gotten up, the opening lines of which read:

O little town of Bethlehem
How fair I see thee lie.

This beautiful poem and book gave me a very good idea of the excellent illustration work Mrs. Eddy had in mind when asking if I could undertake the illustration work for the *Christ and Christmas* poem for her. She also showed me an illustrated poem by Carol Norton which contained two or three illustrations that appeared very good.

I talked with Mrs. Eddy of designs that had begun to come to me, particularly for the first verse:

> O'er the grim night of chaos shone
> One lone, brave star.

Mrs. Eddy approved of my design for this verse without any change. With regard to other verses she advanced some important ideas, one of which aimed to bring out the thought of spiritual Motherhood, another the raising of the dead.

Mrs. Eddy hopefully expressed the desire and confidence that I would put myself wholly in the service of Truth in my efforts, and she expressed great faith in my capacity to do anything that related to this pictorial representation if I trusted in God to guide me. She earnestly quoted to me from the Scriptures: "Trust in the Lord with all thine heart; and lean not unto thine own understanding. In all thy ways acknowledge him, and he shall direct thy paths."[4]

> Pleasant View, Concord, N.H.
> March 20, 1893

My dear Friend

Rejoice with me, the glamour has fled and my noble, loving, good boy, the Dr., is awake and busy doing good. Oh! may he and all of us be delivered from all error or mistakes.

The last illustration of my poem I want to represent storm, lightening and tempest, a palatial home, and a sweet female *beautiful child* in simple garment, bare headed, bare footed, bare-armed, hair disheveled—knocking at the door—of this mansion on Christmas eve.

> Most truly yours,
> Mary B. G. Eddy

The Dr. passed the last sunday with me, went to Boston this morning clothed and in his right mind again. Thank God. I do not believe that the secret mental influence will ever control him again so, but he will be the master.

> M. B. G. E.

> Pleasant View, Concord, N.H.
> March 21, 1893

Mr. J. F. Gilman
Dear Sir:
I would like to see you again, before you make the last sketch.

> Yours truly,
> M. B. G. Eddy
> (per C. A. F.)

> Concord, N.H.
> March 23, 1893

Reverend Mary B. G. Eddy
Dear Spiritual Mother
Your letters indeed caused me to rejoice. I had such a helpless feeling as I cannot describe in words after seeing you Saturday evening. But I am getting to know through experience that it is

according to the workings of spiritual law that this sense of helplessness in the mortal thought shall precede the sense of Truth that is complete and omnipotent in our progress here....

Your suggestion of a last illustration seemed to me very excellent indeed in its main feature, but I felt that it needed something to make it complete which—when I received your second note—I was trusting would appear later, through the same law referred to above by which the sense of void created in our thought through desire and striving for something better and higher is filled from the higher Source without aid from any supposed potency of the lower sense except that the void to be filled has been created through desire and strivings for the higher, impelled by the recognition that the mortal sense is wholly impotent.

Will you write me when you can give me a half hour. I shall need it ere long in order to proceed with the details of your portrait in two or three weeks perhaps.

> Sincerely and only one of thy
> many spiritual sons,
> James F. Gilman

SUNDAY, MARCH 26, 1893

I wrote as follows to Mrs. Eddy:

> Concord, N.H.
> March 26, '93
>
> Reverend Mary B. G. Eddy
> Dear Spiritual Mother
>   I have lately received some new thoughts, or ideas for the illustrations which I have thought you might

like to know of, and consider. A few evenings since I was impelled to study considerably the thought, or idea, in the fourth verse, but apparently without result until I awakened in the night with a new idea (my ideas all seem to come in the darkness). You will remember that the words are:

> Cast thou that brightness Spirit sped,
> That glorious ray
> Which guides the living, wakes the dead,
> To Christ the Way?[5]

Well my idea depends on this view of it: "The glorious ray" is the inspiration of Moses and the Prophets —the Old Testament; the inspiration of Jesus and the Apostles—the New Testament; and the inspiration of *Science and Health,* the final present-ment of the *same* "glorious ray" marking three divisions or eras in which this *one* Light is given to mankind. My idea is to represent in the illustration the Old and New Testament and *Science and Health* as *one volume* or Book, which would emphasize the idea of *oneness* of this *"Ray"* as manifest in Christian or Divine Science with the Light of the Old and New Testaments. Let the illustration be simply a picture of the open Bible, luminous with light, on one side or leaf, indications of Bible Scripture; on the other, of *Science and Health*—our new Scripture.[6] This, it seems to me, quite accurately interprets the *real* thought of the verse; and *suggests* the appropriateness of the classification of Christian and Divine Science, as it has been so grandly and beautifully given us in *Science and Health*, with the elder Scriptures, without saying so, *now,* in so many words, or going so far *yet* as to publish them as one volume or Book. This the world may not be ready for just now. Although many Science students may be, myself for example.

> Christ the idea God appoints
> Of Truth and Life
> The way in Science that anoints
> Life's mortal strife.[7]

It is Love that "anoints life's mortal strife," hence the illustration, I think, should suggest *unselfish* Love strongly. Here is a hint: a school boy of the country district with a younger sister is caught in a blinding snowstorm on his way home from school at night. He bravely protects and cares for the little sister by putting his outer coat from himself upon and around her, and through the blinding snow and blast resolutely draws her home upon his sled. Another: He protects her from a savage big dog where the odds seem greatly against him.

In the last verse of the poem how would a young, beautiful female figure do for a metaphysical interpretation, for I find that kind of an illustration is the only one that will satisfy my thought in this poem. Let the figure be arrayed in simple and appropriate garments standing in a waiting, trusting attitude, facing the reader, in whose whole expression and demeanor is manifest an entire absence of the merely materially personal; and in its place spiritual purity, with Love and Truth and vitality plainly manifest on face and form, with an expression of hopeful yearning for the reader in the expression, but nothing of the suppliant cast. If something in her hand could indicate that she personified Divine Science that would complete it, it seems to me. Success in this illustration would depend on the skill I could command in painting the expression of the qualities I have referred to. Raphael's pictures, the Madonnas, owe their fame to the success with which these qualities were painted particularly the absence of personality they reflect.

Such a picture is worthy of a great effort and successfully painted would be one of the most valuable of pictures.

I cannot tell you how much your brave confidence in my ability to do such a work as these illustrations inspires me to see and understand so much more than I had thought I could. This confidence of Intelligence is what we all need, to do well, to bring out the Real that is our Life, so that men seeing it, shall be compelled to call it good, and bow before it.

Truly yours,
a spiritual son
James F. Gilman

MONDAY, MARCH 27, 1893

Saw Mrs. Eddy on Main Street this afternoon in her carriage when on her daily drive. Stopping her carriage near me, she asked me to call upon her at Pleasant View in the evening. I did so, and we talked of the last illustration referred to above. One of these details related to the book in the hand of the messenger at the door with the word "Truth" upon it. A book was the first thought because Mrs. Eddy's Science was embodied in a great book. The attempt to make use of a book in this connection finally resulted in much laughter on the part of Mrs. Eddy and myself because, by something that was lightly said, it appeared to suggest the call at the mansion of a "book agent." So the book was given up, and a scroll was then thought of and substituted for it. At this interview I sketched Mrs. Eddy's face a little. We looked through an old photograph album and looked at pictures in other parts of the house that resembled Mrs. Eddy "as I used to look," she said. We looked at Milton's statuette and the David bronze, &c.

Pleasant View, Concord, N.H.
March 28, 1893

Mr. James F. Gilman
Dear Sir:

Enclosed please find Mrs. Eddy's check for $60.00 as an installment from her, for labor on illustrations for poem.
Yours truly,
C. A. Frye

Concord, N.H.
March 29, 1893

Dear Spiritual Mother,

Your favor with check for sixty dollars as an installment in advance is duly received. Your liberality and kind consideration is greatly appreciated in return for which I shall greatly endeavor to deserve it in whatsoever I do or undertake. It was as wholly unexpected as it is pleasing or agreeable to my needs, as a portion of it is immediately called for. Please accept my sincere thanks for your faith as much as for what demonstrates it....

Very truly yours,
Jas. F. Gilman

THURSDAY, MARCH 30, 1893

Received a special delivery letter from Pleasant View asking me to call that evening on "business of special importance." Arrived; Mrs. Eddy asked me whether others knew of my presence there that night. She stated that a shadow of hatred and envy attended my presence whenever I came. She said it was not of me.

Mrs. Eddy talked to me of animal magnetism and of its effects and the way to guard against it.

SATURDAY, APRIL 8, 1893

I went up to Pleasant View this evening. Was asked to go up into Mrs. Eddy's sitting room upstairs and saw her there. She greeted me in her kindly, childlike way. I showed her some drawings and sketches of designs, and we talked of what would likely be better and of many other things until 9:30 o'clock.

One of my new sketches represented a design which I ventured to make showing *Science and Health* bound in one volume with the Bible. Mrs. Eddy expressed her disapproval of this, saying such a suggestion now was not in accord with wisdom and was very far from acceptance by the general thought of mankind. "In non-essentials we have always to consider what the general public can accept," she said.

Concord, April 10, 1893

[To Mrs. Eddy]

I shall be ready with some pictures to show, and to ask about some things any time after tomorrow that may suit the convenience of Mrs. Eddy....

Respectfully,
James F. Gilman

Pleasant View, Concord
April 10, 1893

Mr. Gilman

Dear Brother:

Mrs. Eddy desires to see you about pictures. If you will call this eve. she will see you if possible. If she cannot, she will say when she can see you.

In haste,
C. A. Frye

Pleasant View, Concord, N.H.
[April 10, 1893]

Mr. Gilman:

Mrs. Eddy now says she would prefer you to call tomorrow eve. instead of this eve if you will.

C. A. Frye

TUESDAY, APRIL 11, 1893

I went up to Pleasant View and Mrs. Eddy received me in the library and appeared in a sad, long-suffering mood. She began to tell me that God had told her she must give up this thought of illustrating her poem altogether. She said: "You know that when we hear His voice directing us, we must obey it. So now, dear one, put away all thought of any further work on what we have been doing, and also what is already done, and dismiss it entirely from your mind and give your attention to other things. We cannot tell now why this is God's word to us, but later, if we are obedient, we shall know that God's ways are always best for us." I told her as cheerfully as I could that I would do as she requested to the best of my ability. She added: "It has *always* been with me something like this when engaged upon what appeared very good to me to do. God would speak and tell me to give up the form of good work as it appeared to me, and I should know through my obedience a better way for me to do." She gave me her hand and said good-bye to me as if it were the last time we should ever meet.

Of course I felt very down hearted and sorrowful, and this continued for a [time] during which I was seeking to find my

real self for I knew as the sad hours passed that that was my
need and hope, to find my *real self* as Christian Science so abun-
dantly teaches and demonstrates. And so I worked to know that
the goodness of God as the Christ reveals it to us in due time
was all I needed.

THURSDAY, APRIL 13, 1893

The thought came that I would like to write to Mrs. Eddy and
I did so substantially as follows:

> Dear Mrs. Eddy: I have been thinking of many things
> since I saw you and it has come to me that in the case
> of so great and beautiful a poem as yours, there must
> be someone spiritually minded enough so that you
> would feel God's approval in having the poem illus-
> trated. Perhaps the artist in New York who made the
> illustrations for Carol Norton's poem that you showed
> me would be equal to the work. At any rate I feel that
> the work should not be given up simply because I have
> not proved to be spiritually equal to the task.

Concord, April 14 '93

Dear Spiritual Mother

I want to ask you to forgive me, if you can, for my obtuse-
ness and presumptuousness. My eyes seem to have been closed
but now are opened to see the rubbish of personal sense and
self, which, if not cleared out from my mental house renders
impossible the doing of this work for you. One needs be very

clean and white to have anything at all to do with so sacred a work as this, and then the work will go on well and rapidly. What hope is there for one who has every facility and advantage for keeping awake who goes to sleep so often? Will nothing but the rod and prod answer? Let us try again.

It seems plain to me now that the figure representing God's idea should be substantially the same throughout, and that everything of a merely material and literally historical character should be excluded.

Your conception of the figure in the act of healing with arms extended is excellent beyond measure. "O Little Town of Bethlehem" is found very suggestive. I will make some simple outlines of the illustrations with figures and show them to you that the designs may be determined upon before time is spent that might otherwise prove useless, if you approve.

Yours in sincerity and humility,
James F. Gilman

The same day Mrs. Sargent came in the carriage and handed me a note from Mrs. Eddy:

Pleasant View, Concord, N.H.
April 14 [1893]

My dear friend,

Do not feel too much God's dear methods of unfoldment as a rod, but make them a staff.

All is pleasant and hopeful on my side. I have had grace given me to conceive just what you can express

as an artist and have marked it down. God will help
you to do His work.

Lovingly,
Mother

[Mrs. Eddy wrote the following on a sheet of paper
that she enclosed with this letter.]

1
Christian Science Healing
Woman healing the sick

2
Woman and serpent

3
Unity—Christ and woman

4
Knocking

Pleasant View, Concord, N.H.
[April] 15th inst. [1893]

To Mr. Gilman

God will inspire you, if only you follow His *reflection.*

The "window" for this age will let in the true thought to be
delineated—copy it. He has shown me that the 9th verse
should be illustrated by a picture of Jesus pardoning the peni-
tent. Erase the other side note.

Ever lovingly
Mother

SUNDAY, APRIL 16, 1893

Now I was enabled to do this work in a pure sense of the divine goodness in contrast to the self-love and self-complacency that I was tolerating before without consciously knowing it until it had become manifest to Mrs. Eddy's sensitive spiritual thought. The call of God to her was to rebuke it by putting a stop to the work. This became clearer to me at today's interview. Mrs. Eddy appeared very appreciative of the difference between my present thought and that before, saying, after she had talked freely of spiritual things pertaining to the illustration work, "Your thought is *so much better* and purer!" She appeared to rejoice in the simple Christian state of my thought.

Pleasant View, Concord, N.H.
April 23, 1893

Mr. Gilman
Dear Brother:
Mrs. Eddy desires to see you this morning at 9 o'clock or as near that time as you can come and requests that you bring her poem with you.
Yours fraternally
C. A. Frye

Concord, N.H.
April 23, 1893

Dear Faithful Mother
I have been in a dark valley today and have been looking for bearings to ascertain my whereabouts.... What you said this

morning has seemed to unlock to my view a new world of sincerity and reality.

I do not intentionally avoid the performance of any duty that spiritually may be a thrifty growth with me, but something hinders. What is it? That is the question I will steadily ask of God.

Sincerely and very respectfully,
James F. Gilman

FRIDAY, MAY 5, 1893

Mrs. Eddy wrote to me as follows.

Dear friend,

I cannot think of your yielding to malicious minds to such an extent as to turn away from your obligations to me and to your God which are to execute the illustrations as you undertook.

Now dear one do as I say and put down self-will then you will succeed in your undertaking. I send you the poem. It is *greatly* needed by our race and you can illustrate it if you will treat yourself three times each day to the effect that animal magnetism cannot prevent you from carrying out my designs for the illustrations. Do not *think* of *me* in your mental prayer and you must not *fear* that you cannot do this work but *know* that God will enable you to do it. Go *right about it.*

Kindly yours,
M. B. G. Eddy

Remember this, let no one know what you are about.

M. B. G. Eddy

Be careful of this book as I know you will be.

Please call as soon as you read this—something I wish to name to you.

M. B. G. E.

Pleasant View, Concord, N.H.
May 8, 1893

Dear friend,

Please make these changes that come to me inspirationally this morning.

2nd ver. The beams full radiant of the star streaming on the woman,—instead of halo.

3rd ver. An *aged* man in arm chair, not sick, nor infirm, and the little girl that you first had reading to him. Let it represent childhood teaching age from the book S & H.[8]

13 ver. Have a poor-looking candlestick and *candle* instead of lamp (representing the Scripture thought "candle of the Lord") and poverty. Instead of a book in the woman's hand represent her with handkerchief to the eyes as if weeping. The book would present her as "seeking," but hers must be a different thought embodied in this scripture "Blessed are they that mourn for they shall be comforted." Let opposite figure be kneeling but not *bent*. Have beside him a table, and on it a bottle and wine glass and bunch of cigars.

15 ver. Have the figure a woman draped as Jesus is in all the

pictures of him. Have her face solemn, *earnest,* holy. Let the figure express all *we mean.* Have no scroll in her hand but have a halo over her head. The scroll suggests having to label the figure to *interpret* it, and the book S & H occurring so often may suggest an advertisement.

Represent the ideal *woman Christ,* as nearly as possible, let her *delicate* arms, *hands,* and one *little* bare foot be exposed.

6th ver. I want changed. Have it a glorious sunrise and three angels in female forms in the air pointing to this dawn; but have no *wings* on them. Make no specialty of the ground. Have it a sky view.

Now carry out these designs with all the skill of an artist and my story is told in Christian Science, the new story of Christ, and the world will feel its renovating influence.

Do not delay, nor trouble your thought to deviate from what God has given me to suggest, but follow it implicitly, *remember this.*

> Ever yours in Christ.
> Mary Baker G. Eddy

Preserve this copy.

> Pleasant View, Concord, N.H.
> May 8, 1893

Dear Student:

Please make the light from the star which illustrates the first verse much fainter than it is in the second verse.

> With tender regard,
> M. B. G. Eddy

WEDNESDAY, MAY 10, 1893

Had a day's battle with malicious animal magnetism and in the spiritual sense won the day. Moved from room 7 Chapel Street to No. 4 Turnpike St. Such venom as was manifest today was never dreamed of in my general consideration of this subject. It is doubtless occasioned by my connexion with the work of illustration for Mrs. Eddy which is to deal a blow to error in a future day. It appears as a determined obstacle of resistance to this work being carried out.

No. 4 Turnpike St.
Concord, May 10, 1893

Rev. Mary Baker G. Eddy
Dear Faithful Friend and Teacher,

The illustrations are coming on grandly, I think, both in thought or conception and its expression. The suggestions that came Monday, at once appeared just excellent—the very best. Have no concern but I shall strive to carry them out without deviating thoughts of my own.

I have been through one grand day's battle, outwardly, with *malicious animal magnetism* and through God's gracious care, which has been "instant in season" I have been brought through it without a serious wound—and in consequence I am now nicely and quietly located in some upper rooms at No. 4 Turnpike Street (South end). I am isolated *entirely* from those connected with Christian Science labor here and I see that it is best that I should be. I have not been in and out with them since that Sunday five weeks ago that I blundered in making a quotation. I am confident that it was your last solemn charge to me that saved me the day yesterday through my obedience to it. Pitfalls were prepared for me, but just before I came to them God's angel pointed them out to me plainly and I avoided them. Afterwards it was found that those directly engaged in ensnaring me had fallen into the very pitfall prepared for me. The people through whom this awful venom was voiced are uncultivated, hence it was expressed in rudest form. Each time, as soon as it began to manifest itself I saw what it was and was at once impelled to let it come and destroy itself and not try to return it, as it had no power to harm me in the least in a real way. The thought was involuntary that they did not know what they were saying, or doing. I am not sorry for the experience with its glimpse of the horrid monster—this absolute perversion of Truth and Love and Life. I see clearly that it is this work that I am doing in the interest of Truth that occasions it *but it cannot prevail* for I see and realize God's strength sustaining and directing in this work and it guards me from harm. It is God that "fills the famished affections" and God *is more than enough.* I am thankful that once I have been in the spirit of obedience so that I was not betrayed into giving a single thing away that should be kept. It is envy that is at the bottom of it all intensified by many things, one of which is that I keep close as to what I am doing for you, and another that they can bring nothing tangible against me.[9]

Truly Your Earnest student,
James F. Gilman

I shall have two illustrations, the second and third verses, for you to see within a week if you wish to see them. I get my mail at noon and night at the office, *Box 288.*

Truly. J. F. G.

THURSDAY, MAY 11, 1893

I like my two upper rooms at No. 4 Turnpike Street very much. It appears as if God had kindly provided here everything which I have longed for all in one, a condition of things I had been growing to regard as impossible in this material world. The rooms happen to be so situated that views are to be had in three directions—the north, east, and west. At the north are the picturesque roofs and big chimney of an old style New England yellow-brown house with large elms just in front framing in the roof, and woodshed and poultry yard in the rear. At the east is a view of the Merrimac River about a third of a mile distant. Beyond, six miles from the house, are the blue hills of Chichester. The west view is into a picturesque apple orchard and garden. The east window has, besides the distant view and the Merrimac River and meadows, the view of the street where the electric car passes every half hour, also a house just across, where there is a lady who sings sweetly about her housework and plays the piano, but not pretentiously, as yet, at least. They have a dog who is always running out to bark at bicycle riders, also two children of twelve or fourteen years. There is a tin roof just under my workroom windows which makes a fine sounding board for the falling rain and dripping eaves—fine music to me at night—or anytime.

SATURDAY, MAY 13, 1893

Walked up to Bow Mills this morning for a walk. In returning am impelled to make efforts to rebuke in myself all merely material and personal sense of being which Christian Science reveals and demonstrates to be the abnormal and false sense of life which, being temporary, passes away. In the evening walked up to Pleasant View and found Mrs. Eddy was engaged and I returned at once. The evening was so fine, the trees just coming into leaf that I found the walk very enjoyable. The distance from No. 4 Turnpike Street is about a mile and a half.

> Pleasant View, Concord, N.H.
> May 13th [1893]

My dear student,

Your letter gave me comfort. It was just the thing for you to do. "Touch not taste not handle not" (certain persons) is as wise now as when it was written relative to sin in general. God bless your endeavors, they are most important to mankind. If it will be of any aid I will remove my hose from one foot and let you copy it. I used to wear 1½ No. of boot and 5 for gloves or 4½ glove.

Will you give the most defined sense of delicacy in proportions,—and innocence and earnestness and spirituality of expression to the face of figure in verse 2 and the last verse of the poem.

Come and see me Mond. Eve. at 7 oC. Bring all—and I will help you all I can.

> Ever affectionately,
> Mother
> M. B. G. E.

SUNDAY, MAY 14, 1893

Began to feel depressed somewhat. The personal sense is saying to me that the place where I had engaged to take my meals was deficient. Surrounded by strangers and objects not yet accustomed to, I feel sad.

MONDAY, MAY 15, 1893

My feeling of sad depression increased. This morning I felt almost ready to give up my boarding place, so different from the one in the north part of the city.

This evening, having an appointment at Mrs. Eddy's, I go up there over the south-end plain road. Arriving, I tried to postpone seeing Mrs. Eddy until after two or three days, when I should have more to show her in the way of sketches and pictures of designs already determined upon. But she sent back word by Mrs. Sargent, who tends front door, that she wanted to see me. Therefore I remained. She soon came in and greeted me very pleasantly, saying she was glad to see me, with a good deal of unction and feeling, it seemed to me. As soon as she was seated, she began to express a feeling of sympathetic consideration for me, saying that it all seemed strange that I should be set so alone in the world, making pictures as I was, among strangers. I told her I had been feeling depressed and that perhaps she was feeling this. She said with a sober significant look, "You know why you feel depressed, do you not? You were talked up by the Scientists here yesterday, and your feeling is one of the results." I replied that I did not think it was due to that. I told her I supposed she ought to know about it the best, but I had these depressed times often before. But she repeated what she had said before, adding, "I know how things are going; I have heard about it. Your friend (meaning Dr. Foster Eddy) was here yesterday. He went down in that section of the town, and you were talked up. I did not know it until after he was gone, or I should have cautioned him against going there."

In speaking of the way to meet the malicious appearance of evil, she said she "never knew any one who could lump all evil claims together and then meet and demonstrate over them. The *particular* claim of evil that is causing in belief the trouble needs to be singled out in perception and exposed and denied, and up it goes at once." Sometime during this conversation she expressed regret at my having so many troubles and then added: "but then I have all my life been enduring such hardships, and all for good as I have been led later to see."

When we began to talk about the illustrations, she said she had been changing the verses around some and she thought she had made an immense improvement. This she stated with a great deal of interest, and producing the poem, she read me the verses in the order in which she had rearranged them, which placed the verses calling for the illustration of the one rising up out of the casket, second. She said, "I must represent Jesus raising the dead, in the first illustration having a person represented in it. This now places Jesus *first* in the order of the 'illustrations.'" She said, "As it was before, people would say that [I] was giving Christ or Jesus a secondary place; but now he would be placed first, thus rendering him his due."

When she was looking at some of the sketched designs, she laughingly said upon looking at the sketch of the face of the sick man whom she was represented as healing, "There! that man looks just as if he was determined I should *not* heal him." She seemed to recall just that experience in healing. Taken in connection with the expression the man has in the sketch, what she said was decidedly humorous.

In the efforts at designing, and particularly of the one representing the raising of the dead, many comical situations would obtrude themselves unexpectedly, causing much innocent laughter. Mrs. Eddy would say, afterwards, "What would people think if they could see how much laughing attended our trying to pictorially express so solemn a thing as raising the dead?" But the laughing was all of the childlike, innocent kind that expressed divine Love's native joyousness and pure sweet gayety. She said: "Never mind; we shall yet be enabled to get the better of death if we are true to the Life that knows it not."

TUESDAY, MAY 16, 1893

Upon my way home last night I was beset by thoughts that were unfavorable to previous conceptions of Christian Science and Mrs. Eddy, as indeed I was before I went. These thoughts were unwelcome to me, and unreasonable. In the morning, the battle began again, but the enemy was soon routed by the consciousness gained that it was my duty and *privilege* to always see and regard Mrs. Eddy as the perfect image and likeness of the divine spiritual goodness, as a blessed idea of God. I wrote Mrs. Eddy:

Concord, N.H.

May 16, '93

Rev. Mary Baker G. Eddy

Dear Spiritual Mother and Teacher—

I would like to ask if you felt, as from outside influence, unspiritual thought after I came away last evening. I never was quite so much beset by *unwelcome* antagonistic thoughts toward you before as I was last evening and night. It kept me busy with constant denial and affirmation of unquestionable Truth, and apparently all in vain, for I couldn't seem to believe my own words of denial. Everything you said and did seemed to be challenged by what appeared to be my own thought but *it wasn't my thought.* I have found it out. It followed me up with such vehemence that I felt last night as if the solid ground of my understanding was slipping from under me; and that the idea of Christ as an actual reality of Truth, of God, as explained in Christian Science might after all be nothing but a subtle fiction. One thing seemed to hold me and that was the Christ thought as I had *realized* it in self-sacrificing efforts to endure hardship for the sake of His understanding. As soon as I awaked this morning the battle was resumed but soon I gained the victory; and this was it. It is my duty and privilege to *ever behold you as the perfect likeness and image of spiritual Goodness, as the blessed one of God.* Any lesser seeing than this is false altogether because material. These antagonistic thoughts have their source in the general sea of mortal mind, which resists Truth of Spirit as frost resists sunlight; and they reach my consciousness because I am, as yet, in this general sea of mortal mind. The eyes of this seeing cannot reach above matter; and all its seeing is false and illusionary. *Ask no questions of it, for it cannot tell the Truth.*

I have become myself again and have had a very fine spiritual day. Depression has vanished; the beauty of life has reappeared after the dark storm. I am glad I did not try to abolish this darkness by any lesser motive than true good and spiritual advancement, and that you do *not* teach that we should try to do so. I suppose the immediate enemy had more or less of a hand in the voicing of the one evil, but I think, *comparatively* small.

Pictures came on finely today. It has become clear to me that your last improvement in rearranging the earlier verses is very *important indeed.*

> Sincerely and Truly your
> loving and grateful student,
> James F. Gilman

> May 16th [1893]

My dear friend

Be sure and change the hair, have it simply *wavy,* not crisp curls—and a german coil on the back of the head. Be of good *cheer.*

> With love from
> Mother

SUNDAY, MAY 21, 1893

My rooms seem good and my boarding place also, now. We have had a hard rainstorm during the week and it makes fine music in its patter on the tin piazza roof. I am so glad I clung to my boarding place, for it has been *clearly* demonstrated that outward surroundings have little or nothing to do with real happiness. I am confident that *any* surroundings not involving actual deficiency of either food, raiment or seclusion proper to my work would be found agreeable and sufficient if the heart is open to know spiritual things with firm faith to wait upon God and His deliverance.

I took a walk today, over to the Soucook River directly east from Concord, and found it nearer than I supposed, being but about two miles from No. 4 Turnpike Street. Had a long and pleasant walk on the sandy "Plains" on the east of the Merrimac River. The day is warm and sunny with continual winds from the southwest, fragrant with the pitch pines that are there everywhere present. Bathing in the limpid waters of the Soucook River, one is reminded of heaven's purity and the beauty of wholesome, pure thinking as reflected in spiritual obedience.

This day has been truly a Sabbath day to me, although now, at Mrs. Eddy's wise suggestion, I do not attend the C.S. services here. She counsels me to guard my consciousness from others' thoughts.

During the past week I have been making the picture of the illustration "Christian Science Healing," and in particular Mrs. Eddy, as the type of the woman engaged in this picture as healing the sick man. When we were considering the details of the design of the illustration of "Christian Science Healing," the question of what was the most spiritually appropriate disposition of the hands and arms was up for final decision. I reasoned that an attitude of peaceful composure and calmness born of perfect faith in omnipotent Spirit, even perfect understanding of God, should be considered as the most appropriate. I argued that the likeness of the Infinite would realize the perfect reality of all things, hence would have no agitation of mind as to the outcome of the healing thought of Divine Mind and therefore perfect repose and calm in the attitude of the healer should predominate. Mrs. Eddy's reply to this I can never forget. She said: "Yes, *but Love yearns.*"

From this I was led to see that my reasoning was largely the loveless, cold, human, intellectual reasoning that cannot at all see spiritual things in reality, but only the dead literal form of its own vain mortal imaginings.

Mrs. Eddy then took an attitude to express her spiritual

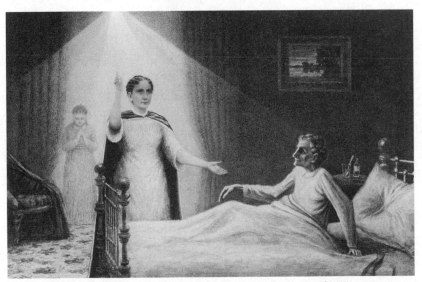

Original drawing for "Christian Science Healing"

concept, to some extent to me. First, she looked upward with a meekly confident, yearning, far-away (from material sense) look and at the same time with her right arm and hand raised with the index finger in a childlike way pointing upward—heavenward. The other arm and hand was stretched out in a downward direction as if toward suffering humanity, appealingly and yet joyously, all in spiritual purity and adoration.

I also worked this week on the child reading *Science and Health* to the old gentleman, illustrating the thought that in Science childhood teaches age because worldly wisdom counts nothing in Truth.

Mrs. Eddy, very soon after the beginning of the illustration work, began to impress upon my thought the great importance of having my mind pure from the thoughts of those about me so far as that thought could be related in any way to my conceptions of God's governing guidance in the work I was entrusted to undertake to do. At first this appeared to be confined mainly to keeping entirely to myself the work on the illustrations I was doing for her. Then, as the time passed, she began to refer to the importance of this in *any* undertaking that was the outcome of pure motives, and especially spiritual aspirations. Mrs. Eddy explained that by keeping our thought *pure* from the conceptions of others until our own individual conceptions had taken, through the Spirit's inspiration, their definitely proper form, we would be giving place *solely* to the formation of the divine perfect Mind, and the results would more nearly correspond to the true ideals actuating us.

In this it was made clear to me that it was not alone in the keeping of spiritual conceptions "hidden in sacred secrecy from the visible world,"[10] that is, from people whom I should judge to be unspiritual in thought until my conceptions should have become fully formulated, but from *all,* however refined they might appear to be to the human sense.

This made plain to me why she included those of her own household (including Dr. Foster Eddy for we have corresponded and he has visited me) in her requests that I keep entirely to myself what I was doing until the proper time should arrive for its presentment. This thought appeared to be universal in its application as she impressed it upon my apprehension. She appeared also to be impelled to *deeply emphasize it* in my case as if she saw I especially needed the injunction, perhaps because she saw then, what she later definitely expressed in saying she found my mentality uncommonly plastic and impressible.

SUNDAY, MAY 28, 1893

A beautiful day, outwardly and spiritually. A day of pleasant memories. I walked up to the park after looking out the Sabbath lesson,[11] about 11 A.M. The air is clear and fresh after the rain of last night, and is laden with the sweet breath of apple blossoms. I remember it is just six months since the day I came to Concord and went, that first day, up back of the park to look the country round and possibly set eyes upon Mrs. Eddy's place. So today I went up to the same place beyond the park, into the by-path leading into the oak shrubbery, and here I saw the beauty of Spirit which the outward world at this time seemed adapted to express. I saw I had a high mission to fulfill.

The value of the pictures is in the spiritual thought they

express, and the joy of this is in the new sense of God which preceding their execution that has made it possible that they shall be thus successful. This new sense has been due to Mrs. Eddy's purity and spirituality. Without that, it would have been simply impossible for me to have made anything of any value whatever in this connexion of illustrating this very spiritual poem. The designs of all the important ones are mainly hers, but in one thing I have contributed to this success and that is in my efforts to be obedient to the spirit of Truth and readiness to try to wake up when I had the least hint that I was getting asleep spiritually, a thing I am prone to do.

It was last Tuesday evening that my picture of the emaciated sick rising at the command of Mrs. Eddy moved her to the feeling remark: "Oh! Mr. Gilman, Mr. Gilman, this is the best piece of work you ever have done." Mrs. Eddy, moved to free expressions of joy says, "God bless you" to me with great feeling. "You are doing a great work in this and still have a great work to do."

Yesterday I was there at 1:30 o'clock P.M. with the picture of the messenger of Truth at the door of the mortal mind mansion. She had brought down a box of pictures of herself to show me that I might gain a good idea of her as she used to be, or look. After I had looked at them, she found that two of them that she wanted particularly to show to me were not there, so she signaled "Laura" and when she came asked her to get them in her room and bring them. Just as she came, I took up that picture illustrating the fourteenth verse of the poem

> Christ calls tonight: 'Oh! let me in!'
> No mass for me.[12]

Original drawing for "Truth versus Error"

to show her. This picture is the one she has wanted should be the most impressive, and I was feeling I had succeeded so well, that I felt confident she would like it. The conception and execution of it had come to me this past week since Tuesday evening, when I was striving harder than ever before to *realize* my true normal manhood in God, as Christian Science teaches and to keep from falling into the drowsy mesmeric sleep as related to spiritual consciousness which Mrs. Eddy, last Tuesday evening, showed me I was continually doing.

As soon as Mrs. Eddy's eyes rested upon the picture, she was very still for a moment and then she said, "Laura, look here! look at that picture!" I began to fear that it looked dreadful to her on account of the exposed shoulder and breast, especially when Laura began to say, "Oh! Why, Mother, Mother," but adding, "Isn't that beautiful! beautiful!" Mrs. Eddy echoed her words, and they both were in that joyousness that sometimes finds expression in tears and Mrs. Eddy was saying, "It is the perfect representation of the ideal I had in thought, but could not exactly describe."

Afterwards, when Laura, still having the pictures in her hand that she had brought down, holding them toward Mrs. Eddy, said, "Here are the pictures you wanted." Mrs. Eddy said, "We don't want them now. He has got the picture perfect." After this I went up to her room when she was ready—her sitting-room chamber, where she writes and attends to her daily work—and sketched her foot for this same picture, a place being left in the picture for that to be done according to a previous arrangement. When I came to go, she considerately remembered to come to the door with me and give me her hand in a good-bye and "God bless you."

SUNDAY, JUNE 4, 1893

Last Thursday evening I was up at Pleasant View again. I had written Mrs. Eddy on Tuesday, two days before, of my need of means to meet my material necessities, having entirely exhausted my supply in hand, including $20.00 I had borrowed. On Wednesday Mr. Frye wrote me Mrs. Eddy desired me to come up Thursday 12:30 P.M. or evening for answer to my letter. She arranged to supply me weekly with means sufficient to meet my current expenses. She proceeded at once to talk of my call for material means, and asked me how much my expenses amounted to per week. I replied, stating a reasonable sum per week, enough to meet current expenses for each week including a little for incidentals, such as artist's materials.

At this interview she asked me not to think of her personally at any time, saying that my thought, or atmosphere of mind, being unspiritual, interfered with hers and her work. There was no objection to my thinking of her in the spiritual way that is natural upon reading her works, and I see plainly there is no objection to thinking of her in any way that harmonizes with the spiritual sense of being which her teachings inculcate.

FRIDAY, JUNE 9, 1893

Mrs. Eddy wrote me as follows.

> Dear friend,
>   I forgot the stipend last evening—and will hand it to you in one week when you next call. God bless you and cheer you and uplift to the joys of heaven.
>   Mother

THURSDAY, JUNE 15, 1893

This evening I was up to Mrs. Eddy's with a single picture to show that I had mostly spent the four days of the week illustrating the verse containing the lines:

> Who can portray the heavenly worth
> Of that high morn?[13]

In this illustration, in fulfillment of Mrs. Eddy's design, was to be two angels moving swiftly through the air to welcome the approaching dawn. These angels were not, according to Mrs. Eddy's idea, to be delineated in the usual conventional way as having *feathered* wings, an ideal that Mrs. Eddy objected to as being unnatural and confusing. The problem to the artist in such a case was, how to picture them as angels to the eyes of observers who have only known pictures of them as angels by the possession of wings wherewith to fly. I labored and struggled with this problem some days.

I had represented the figures of the angels as best I could without wings as rising swiftly upward through the air toward the light, with long light drapery covering the figures except the head and arms. I indicated their swift passage through the air by the fluttering of the light drapery that enshrouded them; the darker hair of their heads causing the heads to appear the main part of the figures in the picture as viewed from a distance. Upon seeing my effort, Mrs. Eddy laughing, kindly asked me where the angels were. I frankly answered as if her question was intended to be regarded seriously, pointing to the figures I had drawn to represent the angels. "Oh, are those the angels? I thought they were tadpoles." She then said, laughing compassionately, "Now, that is too bad to say that, isn't it, Mr. Gilman?"

An important thought that was advanced during the evening was that God provides for a *testing* of us which we shall realize sharply if we progress spiritually fast. The more rapidly we progress, the more sharply we shall be tested. She said she was almost destitute of the bare necessities of life during the first four years of her practice in Christian Science because "I thought then the healing work ought to be gratuitous as it was in Jesus' day." I asked her if it did not seem as if God failed to provide at that time. She replied that "God provided the testing that I then needed." She said that God was testing me now through my sense of poverty, and if I endured the testing faithfully, then would follow abundance as it had in her case.

Mrs. Eddy after this said she had a picture with two angels in it that she liked, all except the wings. Perhaps I could get some idea from that that would help me to express the spiritual thought she had in mind. So she had Mrs. Sargent get it from another room where it hung framed. The picture was a spiritual and very beautiful one, and it gave me the idea that I needed, which I modified by leaving the wings out for one thing and making the rest of the picture to suit the high requirements of Mrs. Eddy's thought.

Mrs. Eddy said shortly before I went, thinking perhaps I would feel disheartened, that God would surely help me to do my work, and "God bless you."

FRIDAY, JUNE 16, 1893

I began to have the feeling named by Mrs. Eddy "chemicalization,"[14] and it was the severest I believe I ever experienced. The day was veritably a "black Friday" to me. In my thought I was seeking to endure the mental testing for the Truth's sake. It appeared to beget a feeling that spirituality and heaven were *terribly costly.*

SATURDAY, JUNE 17, 1893

This morning I felt some better. In the forenoon Mr. Frye brought me a letter from Mrs. Eddy.

> Dear friend,
>
> I feel that the Divine Love bids me write to you and waken you from the dream of sense. This delay to do the illustrations of an important Poem is caused alone by mortal malicious mind which in scriptural language is *enmity* against God, *good.* You can and must rise from this condition and complete your agreement with me within the space of three weeks. The time that has been lost by repeating your experiments was the fruits of disobedience to spiritual ideas. Now abide alone by my instruction and *watch* and pray constantly against "spiritual wickedness" the power of darkness, and the efforts of persons to keep you from consummating your work.
>
> I shall not continue to entreat you and pay you as much in vain as hitherto, but I shall demand of you to *earn* the sums that I am paying you, and when you rise from this glamour of the senses superinduced by evil you will thank me for this and see your obligations *morally* and *fulfill them.*
>
> The word "Truth" should be put on the scroll in the hand of the figure illustrating the last verse. No other scroll should appear.
>
> As ever your faithful friend,
> Mary B G Eddy

This letter did not have the effect to agitate me, perhaps because I had already begun to rise out of the dark valley toward the uplands that her letter would spur me to try to reach. This evening, light dawned upon me:—It showed me it was divine Love alone that illumines our way and made our tasks light, and seeking to know for a certainty that I *love* God was what I ought to labor for more—with love as dominant in my thought all would be light.

MONDAY, JUNE 19, 1893

I wrote to Mrs. Eddy as follows.

> Dear Faithful Friend:
> I believe a New Day has dawned to my under-standing, and will so appear as time passes.
> I *see* that it is Love alone that illumines the Way, and is the one inspiration of true righteousness; the Light of Truth in which is no darkness or uncertainty. *Love motive is the only power,* and *it is sufficient,* and it is available to us all.
> Great favor and privilege is vouchsafed to me. That my works shall prove that I desire God supremely is my earnest hope.
> > Gratefully and obediently,
> > Yours Truly
> > James F. Gilman

Immediately after this peculiar dark period of conflict with evil belief which was followed by the new dawn of Truth's light as above narrated, I was walking toward Bow Mills, about sunset. In this walk I was still naturally in my freshly attained chastened sense, and therefore more ready to hear and see spiritually. The sky was mostly cloudy, but a break in the clouds in the west occurred as I walked, so that the sundown rays of light streamed through, causing a sharp cupola that was on a building just in line with me and the sunset rays of light, together with some beautiful trees, to appear silhouetted against the light western sky in a very picturesque, artistic way. Immediately the spirit of Truth said to me, "There, that is what is wanted in the picture with the angels to represent 'the heavenly worth of that high morn.'"

THURSDAY, JUNE 22, 1893

I received this note from Mrs. Eddy and went to see her.

> Dear friend,
>   Your kind note at hand. Am glad you report progress spiritually[;] this is the one thing needed by us all on our way to heaven.
>   Please call tonight if you get this in time. If not tomorrow eve. Come bearing your sheaves with you. May heaven's blessing rest on you.
>   Very truly,
>   M. B. G. Eddy

When I showed the new illustration to Mrs. Eddy, she at once expressed great joy because the spiritual beauty of the whole picture expressed her sense of the verse in the poem it

"Christmas Morn" and the helpful picture of the angels with wings

was intended to illustrate, and she asked for no change to be made in it. In the finished illustration, the spire of the little church is made higher than the cupola on the building to suit poetic requirements, but it was the product of the ideal God gave me in nature to supply my need for getting a suitable illustration for the poem.[15]

June 1893

Bring the illustration of the woman and serpent and I will tell you how it *must* be *altered,* also bring, *Ascension.*
M B G Eddy

FRIDAY, JULY 1, 1893

In response to an invitation from Mrs. Eddy to come up to lunch today at noon, I went up at the appointed time and was pleasantly welcomed and ushered into the library by Mrs. Sargent to await the appearance of Mrs. Eddy. Soon a gentle rustling from the heavily carpeted stairway foretold her coming and as she appeared in the open doorway; her face was radiant with an earnest and smiling welcome. She advanced with extended hand and greeting of goodwill, saying she was sorry that she could not see me the evening before. The day was exceedingly warm. Through the open window came the westerly summer wind, cooling and comforting in its fragrance. By the window was an easy chair toward which she advanced, asking me at the same time to "find a comfortable seat this warm day," then adding, "here, take this chair here by the open window."

I replied, "I have been sitting there a little after I first came in; there is a fine breeze there, and so it is just the place for you to sit." She would not hear to this, but answered with a smile, saying, "I know it, and that is why you must sit here." Her command was pleasantly imperative. It could not be successfully withstood, and I yielded.

Immediately she pointed out to me a beautiful flower growing out on the lawn—a single stalk with a single flower, noting it had done better than it promised in the early season. I had been looking out of the window before she came down, but I had not seen the flower and its beauty then. I replied in accord with what I now saw. I said: "It looks beautifully sweet and courageous in its loneliness I think." "Doesn't it?" she replied with much feeling. She added, "That is the way it is in spiritual living—in Christian Science, often. Oh," she continued, "how often I have found myself standing entirely alone with God, standing for the right—for His word—with everyone striving to pull me back, offering every inducement to go some other way. How much I would have given sometimes if I only could have had some one to talk with, some one who knew more than I did. But that could not be to the pioneer. And not only in this mental way, but outwardly as related to my necessities. I stood alone in the first years of my demonstrations of Spirit's supremacy. Oh, Mr. Gilman," she exclaimed with much emphasis and expression, "I sometimes used to wonder, 'Why does not God provide for my needs.' I who was raising the incurably sick (to medical sense) to health and strength so speedily as to cause amazement, even from death's door; and in the families of the wealthy. Yet I was often hungry for the want of simple things that I craved, ordinarily considered necessities of life, because I lacked the material means for obtaining them. But God in His graciousness was testing me, that was all.

"You see," she added, "at that time I thought it would be wrong to take anything for doing such Christly work. I thought it was a gift from God to be able to heal as Christ healed and that I ought not to take money for it. Christ did not. I worked and healed four years in this way, without money and without price; and then, God having tested me, He showed me a better way." I said, "I think your very delicacy and sensitiveness in this matter was an essential part of your qualification for healing, and for being God's messenger to the world, waiting in hungry need for the message; because of the spiritual perception of the incongruity of a money or material recompense for spiritual blessings bestowed." "That was it," she answered in artless simplicity.

Continuing, she said, "You remember my recent article on Spring[16] in the *Journal?* Do you remember there was a verse in the latter part? Well, someone composed a piece of music for just that one verse alone…. Well, I have composed some more verses to go with it, and I will have Mr. Frye bring me them, and I will read them to you." Waiting for this, she added, "I used to write poetry for adaptation to music and for publication in periodicals. It used to be natural to me; I could compose without serious effort. It was the same with drawing and music. I was passionately fond of things like these, which I did not need to learn as others did, but I had a more important work to do than any of these. So I was kept from accomplishing much in any of these ways; something unexpected would always seem to come up to prevent."

I replied, "The essence and beauty of them all and more, is condensed in the book you finally wrote—*Science and Health*—was it not?"

"Oh, indeed that was it; we can see it now," she said, adding, "When I was at school, very young, I used to say when the subject in our play came up as what we were going to be or do, that I was going to write a book. It was not books, but a Book that I was going to write."

The verses having been brought, she proceeded to read them to me in a sweet, earnestly expressive voice, beginning as follows:

Oh! gentle presence, peace and joy and pow'r
Oh! Love divine that owns each waiting hour,
Thou Love that guards the nestling's falt'ring flight!
Keep Thou my child on upward wing tonight.[17]

Mrs. Eddy then read me the additional verses which she had told me before she had very recently written. She referred to the rhythm of the poem as being of that cadence which more readily reaches and appeals to the ear of the popular thought than most of her other poems. She later referred to the lines:

only with mine eye
Can I behold the snare, the pit, the fall

in explanation to me that "mine eye" in this line referred to the mortal personal sense eye which only can see the evil delusions of matter belief. She kindly loaned me a copy of the whole poem as now written.

Soon after lunch I went up in the room over the library called "Benny's room" ("Benny" is a pet abbreviation from "Ebenezer,"

Dr. Foster Eddy's Christian name) where Mrs. Eddy said we could go to attend, free from interruption, to the perfecting of some designs and drawings relating to the illustration "Seeking and Finding" which she was much interested in. At this time the question was as to the position of the hand on which the head of the woman in the picture was lightly resting. To get this more surely accurate, Mrs. Eddy consented to sit as a model with her head resting lightly against her hand as in the illustration. After I had sketched the main line of her face and figure with the hand resting against the head, I felt the need of her position being just a little different, so little that I thought best not to ask her to rise and move lest she move too much, and so I took the few steps to where she was sitting and said to her that if she didn't object I would like to move her just a little. She smiled but didn't object and I took hold of the chair in which she was and did my best to lift the chair a little including the occupant. I could lift a hundred pounds of grain easy, but I found I could not lift or move Mrs. Eddy.

SUNDAY, JULY 9, 1893

At lunch on July 1 a large saucer of fresh, ripe strawberries was served from the Pleasant View garden. Although I was fond of strawberries, I found myself obliged to leave the major part of this dish of strawberries uneaten. A few days afterwards, when the question of the capacity of spiritual things to satisfy our needs was referred to, I said to Mrs. Eddy that I had noticed that when I was present at lunch with her and she was verbally expressing many spiritual things, that I felt an absence of desire for food, not usual with me, however attractive it might ordinarily have appeared to me, and that I had thought about this. It had come clear to me that what we really all hunger for is a sense of real love and Truth, the good that we desire to receive, and that alone feeds and sustains us truly and this more perfectly than the literal food, however good, ever can.

To this Mrs. Eddy responded warmly that I had the true thought with regard to real food and appeared much gratified that I had thus spiritually perceived the Truth.

The beautiful thoughts of the poem that begins "Oh! gentle presence" continues to make music in my head and heart.

Mrs. Eddy seems spontaneously to discern error and sin in the mortal thought, even though cunningly covered under the semblance of good, but which is, after all, nothing but some form of self-love. This has been illustrated in my experience with Mrs. Eddy so many times now.

I had finished pretty nearly two of the pictures that seemed to her very important; and I had succeeded "wonderfully," she said. She liked them so well that she showed them to the other members of the household. The expression on the faces in the pictures was an important part to get. She liked what I accomplished in that way very much with some slight exceptions, which she said she was afraid to have me undertake to correct lest I injure the parts she did like.

I knew I could make the corrections she referred to; and I also felt that there was much more I could do to improve them. "Well," she said, "you be very careful." In this, the satisfaction and joy I seemed to be the occasion of, fanned my self-love, I think, so that the all-sufficiency and inclusiveness of God's love and my great need and necessity for spiritual reliance was lost sight of in the foolish belief that I, the mortal, was being of service to Christian Science in my ability as an artist. Its effect was not to make me *outwardly* less obedient to Mrs. Eddy's word, but unconsciously less heedful of the spiritual sense of God's word and guidance, and so to strive in the fancied strength of material sense and my art mastery to seek to excel what I already had done that was satisfactory.

I thus worked diligently a whole day in making supposed improvements, and thought I had succeeded well. Toward evening I took them up for inspection, but Mrs. Eddy was out upon her usual drive, so I left them. The next day a letter, with a vigorous superscription, was mailed to me—the only letter I have received from Mrs. Eddy superscribed in her own hand, although she always writes her letters. It read:

> Pleasant View, Concord, N.H.
> July 7, 1893
>
> Dear Mr. Gilman,
>   The last illustration is *not done* as I requested. The second illustration you have spoiled! unless you can recover your lost art. Do not do thus with the others. Come to me *once* more prepared to do as you said you would, "make the changes in my house."
>   In haste.
>   M. B. G. Eddy

I am out for a drive from 3 to 5 P.M. At half past twelve is the best time to see me.

I had expected a vacation this month, the first in
26 *years!* but find none so far.

Before receiving this letter I had gone up to her house in
the interest of some other pictures I was finishing. (I neglected
the getting of my mail in the morning that day, hence was not
"prepared" with my brushes as the letter had directed me to
be.) I went in the supposition that she would be pleased with
the pictures as corrected. But she received me very coldly and
began at once to express displeasure, asking why I persisted in
disobeying her express commands.

Mrs. Eddy continuing, said that it seemed as if her students
were obsessed to do the very things she had commanded them
not to do: as if animal magnetism *or* sin, (she emphasized this),
was leading them by some fate to undo or spoil whatever of
good they chanced through her efforts to do at other times, by
their willingness to be thus led. She would not see the other pic-
tures I had brought up, but commanded me to go back to my
rooms until Monday, (it was now Saturday, 2 P.M.), and not to
do a single thing in the intervening time, and then come up
again prepared to correct my bad work. Then she left me with
a cold good day.

I went away feeling then partly amused in my kindly disposed
personal sense way at being treated so much like a mother's boy,
and by such a great mother too, for I did not believe I had greatly
injured the pictures. A touch about the eye or mouth will change
a picture so much, which she could not realize. (She said one of
the faces looked now "as if in a fit of apoplexy;" she had "seen
them look exactly like that.") Still, I soon felt sobered by the

thought that I had probably been very conceited and careless in working so much upon pictures that had already seemed to please so well. This thought grew upon me, and my vanity and self-conceit began to appear and a sense of my great folly, until I could scarcely sleep that night. Her word and thought always grows upon me when I get away from her personal presence.

I wrote her a letter that night in which I said:

> Concord, New Hampshire
> July 8, 1893
>
> Dear Mother
>
> I know that God will reproduce the good that seems to have vanished through thoughtlessness.... His rainbow of promise spanned the sky just at the last tonight when I was looking to Him for relief from despair.
>
> My seemingly vain and bitter regrets which I have been struggling with this afternoon gather their bitterness from the fact that you and your college students have been possibly robbed of that which would have been prized very highly but for a dreadfully careless and profane hand of mine, the most regrettable thing I could ever imagine myself as doing. But I am feeling that God will not forsake us now; and that He will yet give us as good or better than we had before. This has been my usual experience in similar circumstances in times past. What helps me the most is the faith that destroys fear. If this lesson only sinks deep enough in my heart so that it shall abide it will do much good. I am thinking my case is pretty nearly

hopeless. I ought to cope more earnestly and success-
fully with mortal mind than I do, that is surely so.

> With new hope I remain your
> would-be disciple in Truth.
> James F. Gilman

I had not received your letter when I was with you today.

I find that my experience in this was almost exactly like that
described in the first of the three stages in "Pond and Purpose"
by Mrs. Eddy.

MONDAY, JULY 10, 1893

This morning, I felt renewed and refreshed, and with a chas-
tened sense I went up again, this time prepared, and with my
brushes, as she had before requested. I was ushered into the
library as usual and awaited with confidence born of Spirit,
Mrs. Eddy's appearance. Soon I heard the gentle rustle on the
stairs that I had learned to know, followed by her appearance
in the doorway. Instantly, I felt that she perceived the state of
my mind upon seeing me as I arose and advanced a step to
meet her and clasp her extended hand of welcome. She
retained the hold upon my hand as she stood close to me in her
precious way, and looking very earnestly and with solicitation
up into my eyes, she said yearningly like a mother, "It seems
hard to bear, I know. You won't feel hard toward me, will you?
I felt I must be severe because you needed it; but it was hard
for me to be so." I was striving to restrain the floods that
threatened to inundate me. I finally found voice to say that

there was nothing but gratitude in my mind for her faithfulness toward me, to which she joyfully responded, "I am so glad!"

"Oh!" she said with great feeling, "You don't know what burdens I have bourn through the necessity I have felt for rebuking students, but who could not receive my rebuke as coming from true love for them. This is the great test of the true student. If they are found unwilling to bear this test, they are not worthy to be found in this work. It is the resentment that rebuke uncovers or excites that makes up the burden—*the terrible burden* that I have had, and still have to bear in this pioneer work of Christian Science. It was nothing but a constant joy to me to minister to the needs of humanity in the healing work. It was when I began to teach and be faithful with students that I began to know of suffering and sorrow."

I was glad to be able to say this time I had cherished no resentment toward her because of her rebuke and had accepted from the first the fact that I needed it, even if I did not see where, and that it surely would do me good which I should surely see in due time. To this I added that now I was so glad I had looked at it in that way, for I had gained one experience in particular in this that I valued greatly. I found that this sorrowful suffering enabled me to realize spiritual love for others without regard to their attainments of goodness or deficiencies.

"Yes," she responded, "it is through the suffering that God had called me to pass through that I have been enabled to realize God's Love as I have."

I told her that I was feeling sure that God would reproduce again the value that seemed to be in the picture before, to which she hopefully and cheerfully responded: "God will surely help you to do it, and you will be able to in His strength." She appeared now to have no concern about this or regret at the loss the pictures seemed to have sustained, but told me I could be alone in the room upstairs, free from interruption. "When you want me, come to my door and knock—until eleven o'clock." She added after a little pause, laughingly, "I will not be knocked at by anybody after that until lunch time." I judge this to be to her a sacred hour.

The correction of the pictures came on finely, and she said at lunch time upon seeing them, that she liked them better than before.

Have received $108 altogether from Mrs. Eddy for illustration work.

[July 1893]
Wednesday

My dear friend,

Be sure and not leave the hair on the figure of last illustration[18] of the poem in a set curl but only very slightly waved at the ends.

Also make the illustration of the second verse[19] *older* looking—all of 30 years old. Give more *strength* to the mouth and *soul* to the *eyes*.

Most truly,
M B G Eddy

MONDAY, JULY 17, 1893

At Mrs. Eddy's during the forenoon working in "Benny's" room with Mrs. Eddy in the work of perfecting the illustrations—the more important ones, such as "Seeking and Finding" and

"Christian Unity." In this perfective work Mrs. Eddy empha-
sized one thought, not only at this particular time but at several
other times. She would say very impressively, as apparently little
things which when done appeared to improve the illustration,
"Trifles make perfection, but perfection is no trifle." She attributed
this saying to Raphael, but appeared to think it worthy of a deep
impression upon our sense of doing worthy work. After lunch
Mrs. Eddy was ready for her drive just about a minute after my
own departure. Before I had had time to get quite to the high-
way, I heard her voice calling to me from her carriage which she
had just entered. I returned and she invited me to get in with her
and ride. I felt pretty highly honored and grand riding with the
beloved Mrs. Eddy in her private carriage.

TUESDAY, JULY 18, 1893

Left some pictures at the *Concord Monitor* office to be engraved
for Mrs. Eddy's poem. All of the illustrations are not done yet,
but Mrs. Eddy is seeking to get the poem with its illustrations
into publication form in time to have it at the World's Fair at
the time of the Congress of Religions in September or early in
October. The task devolves upon me, at Mrs. Eddy's request, to
attend to the having of the pictures photographed. In this part
of my work I found manifest the usual resistance to the spir-
itual thoughts and work of Mrs. Eddy, but not fully at first. It
appeared mainly to be confined to the chief platemaker and was
made manifest at first by insinuating questions with regard to
the illustrations and their relation to Christian Science and
Mrs. Eddy. Finally it came out to him that Mrs. Eddy objected

to my placing my signature on any of the illustrations. This appeared to arouse his antagonism to Mrs. Eddy and Christian Science to more positive expression in which he indicated that this objection of Mrs. Eddy to an artist signing his own work confirmed his previous opinion of what Mrs. Eddy really was. But I wouldn't hear anything like this.[20]

THURSDAY, JULY 27, 1893

I wrote to Mrs. Eddy as follows.

> Dear Mother:
>
> I went in and talked with Mr. Pearson[21] this afternoon, and he has fully assured me that these illustrations shall be all right and *to please you,* and quite as well and probably better than the ones of your place that you like so well. He has given me authority to have these illustrations *made to suit me,* to look after the progress of the plates as closely as I desire, and to criticize freely; and have them taken over again until first class plates are obtained. He wants I should do this. He says he desires to make this a test job of what they can do in a first class way. He has purchased some special type for this poem that he believes you will like. So dear Mother please dismiss all anxiety on account of this work for *I can see it is going to be done right.*
>
> He says Mr. Bowers had an hundred printed on extra fine paper of the "Pleasant View" picture of which the one you sent down by me today was one,

but he says the paper for your poem is nicer than that paper for the printing and also, of course, vastly thicker. There is no lurking antagonism in Mr. Pearson's thought; that is sure, and I found [the chief platemaker] in a very different frame of mind when I called there this P.M. probably on account of Mr. Frye's taking the three pictures away, just before. I shall probably have something to show you ("fierce heart beats") Saturday next at 1:30 P.M. if it does not rain.

Yours Truly and gratefully,
James F. Gilman

SATURDAY, JULY 29, 1893

Called with some proofs of "Unity" and "Treating the Sick," at Mrs. Eddy's. I was asked to come up to her sitting room. Found her sad. She spoke of her travail of soul: she had labored to bring forth to the world a C. S. Artist &c. She could not undertake another such work. I told her I had begun to see as I never had seen before how much I was indebted to her. Told her that the testing had shown me how feeble I was spiritually; that I had doubts sometimes if I really believed in God.

THURSDAY, AUGUST 3, 1893

Went up and across lots and saw Mrs. Eddy at the boathouse. Found her in a happy frame of mind. We went into the new boathouse and she had some new ideas to be carried out in the pictures. The last illustration she said must be a representation of the Ascension. We deliberated whether it would be best to have the central figure a woman, or to represent Jesus. It was decided that the time had not quite come for the woman to be represented in such a picture. To be too fast in such a case, with even one illustration, would be to spoil the good effect of the whole work, Mrs. Eddy said.

When I was working up the design of "Healing the Sick," I took the liberty to introduce in the background light that was streaming in some faintly presented children's faces after Raphael's idea in the picture of "The Sistine Madonna." Mrs. Eddy finally did not approve of these in the picture and I removed them. Now Mrs. Eddy recalled the thought of these child faces and said to me that in the Ascension picture I could put in the child faces. She thought in this picture they would be very appropriate.

I went back to my rooms and sketched out the design of the Ascension as I felt the inspiration to do in accord with her thought and suggestion. I succeeded so well that I went up with it after dinner directly to show to her. Mrs. Eddy was having an interview with some Scientist from the far West. I waited out on the south verandah until she soon came inquiring for me. She asked me up to her sitting room and looked at the design and thought it excellent. She referred to what she had been talking of with the Scientist; did so merely because her mind seemed to be full of that thought and it thus became natural to speak of it. She said malicious animal magnetism had been trying all over the land to precipitate evil, leading into all sorts of sin and destruction, seeking to lay its work to Scientists, but said she, "I have been holding it back." She spoke in such a way that I did not feel that I understood and that perhaps I ought to. So I said, "Is it something I may inquire about? I do not just understand what you mean. Do you mean that some particular individuals that you know are seeking to do these things?" This seemed to vex her a little, and she replied, "You know the use of language, don't you? I don't see how the language can make it any plainer." She went on to say that mesmerism sought to make people believe that they hadn't any mind at all and that therefore they could not exercise their mind. I asked if she meant that idiocy belief was thereby induced. She replied that she had known of subjects becoming mesmerized into the belief of complete idiocy. She said she did not recognize these powers as realities; did not allow it to have a place, or give it a name in her consciousness.[22]

SATURDAY, AUGUST 5, 1893

Friday afternoon and today all day I worked on Mr. Runnels'[23] Lake Sunapee pictures to get them done, but did not get the last one (the cover) done. I had told Mrs. Eddy I would be up again soon with proofs from the *Concord Monitor* office, but as there was none yet made and I had nothing to show of work on the Ascension picture, I didn't go up. I felt she would be expecting me and annoyed that I did not come, as she had enjoined me to hasten, but Mr. Runnels' work could not wait as the season was quickly passing when he could get any return from it. It had been begun when it was supposed that I could attend to the work, &c. I also was in the need of some income.

SUNDAY, AUGUST 6, 1893

Mr. Frye came for me with a carriage. Said Mrs. Eddy wanted I should bring the Ascension picture and also the candle-lighted picture. He would carry me up. So I took the sketch transfer which was all I had done to it since I had seen her and went up with Mr. Frye, expecting nothing but rebuke and storm. The candle-lighted picture with the woman with handkerchief to her eyes was at the *Monitor* office, so being Sunday, we could not get it. It was this that she began at once to talk about, saying that this must be changed. "The idea of the woman weeping was wrong." I began to try to persuade against this idea because it had seemed to please her so, and I had taken such pains to finish it nicely. I thought that likely her thought was temporary. She immediately began to rebuke me, saying peremptorily, "You just stop! Stop at once! I won't hear it! Why will you persist in resisting and disobeying me. In consequence you don't get the picture as it should be, which occasions all this delay," &c. I showed her the transferred sketch showing the improvement over the first sketch and then went, in obedience to her direction, back to the getting of the change made and the last one done as soon as possible.

TUESDAY, AUGUST 8, 1893

Went up to Mrs. Eddy's today at 1 o'clock p.m. Mrs. Sargent met me at the door, her face all smiles, saying, "Oh, I am so glad you have come," by which I knew Mrs. Eddy was in the happy mood agreeable to the human sense of being. Mr. Frye and

Mrs. Sargent in particular are faithful reflectors to my sense of Mrs. Eddy's state of mind. I had with me the picture representing Mrs. Eddy at the table with the candle at night, which she liked some at first and afterwards very much after I had made some changes under her supervision in Benny's room upstairs.

She said soon after I came that she had prayed for me. I replied that I needed it badly enough, and truly this had been so during the few days past because of more conflicts with self I had been passing through in which I had felt somewhat rebellious at the thought of becoming *completely* subject to Mrs. Eddy's direction as now seemed inevitable. The thought that clarified it somewhat being this: that Jesus' disciples left all to follow him, and plainly would not have been worthy to have been called disciples if they had not. Paul, whom I have admired so much, did more than this. How could I complain if I was called to do the same in giving up completely self-will. I believe now that I can see that she had been bringing self-will to the surface in my case that she might destroy it, for that was where my battle had been. She had told me Sunday morning when I came up, having ridden up with Mr. Frye, not to let self-will govern me. Monday she consoled me saying regretfully that she *had* to talk to me severely the day before for my good, holding my hand tenderly as she said it. She added that she had to talk to herself in the same way, "or rather," she added, "I used to do so," as if now it was not necessary.

Today while she was sitting just at my right and a little behind, watching and suggesting as the changes were made in the picture, she said, after some visitors from Boston who were looking over the place had looked into the room where we were and had gone, "These rooms will all be interesting to visitors after I am gone." Then she added, "I ought to be gaining the victory over death, hadn't I? That is what I have been preaching."

I said what an immense work that would be! I then asked her, "What constitutes a victory over death? Is it to live in this life perpetually?"

She said, "No; at least not to be visible to mortals to much extent. We overcome death when we fully overcome material sense and that then it is not able to behold us because Spirit is not appreciable to matter." I said I suppose that in that stage of advancement we shall still have a body that will be just as real to us as this body. "Not in a finite personal way," she said. I said I could not separate in my thought the idea of my identity from its embodiment in some form.

"That is true," she said, "Your identity will have its embodiment, but it will not be finite in form and outline like this personal body. I think of our existence in that state more as we think of one who in some crisis rises to vigorous, noble action that is characteristic of that one's nature. We do not think of a person's body at such times, but of the force of mind, of the spiritual import."

I asked, "Do you think Paul ever saw Jesus?" She answered, "No, not the personal Jesus." I said, "He says he saw some one 'above fourteen years ago whether in the body or out of the body I cannot tell.'" "Yes, I know," she said, "but the personal Jesus had been done away with because Jesus had advanced beyond the personal sense of things, hence there could have been no such embodiment at that time." I said, "Perhaps the followers and disciples of Jesus were holding the sense of the personal Jesus so strong in their thought that that became the embodiment of Jesus to Paul, which was what Paul saw and referred to." "Yes, it might have been that," said she, "I have had letters from people saying they had seen me bodily and that I had healed or helped them, but of course they couldn't have seen me in the ordinary way, for I knew nothing of it."

She pointed to a low rocking chair without arms, old-fashioned mahogany, with hair seat, saying, "In that chair I wrote *Science and Health*." I said, "It is a very valuable chair." "Yes," she replied. "The world will cherish all those things in future time."

MONDAY, AUGUST 14, 1893

Thursday went up with "Ascension" to Mrs. Eddy's so far as I had gotten it along, to show her, to see how she liked my conceptions of her ideal. I had made the children's heads in the light background with the lower ones full formed, not distinct, but arms and nude cherub bodies strongly suggested, but not actually outlined definitely on the right of the picture. She looked at it and at once expressed approval without critically examining the forms separately. After receiving Mrs. Eddy's approval, I worked diligently on these forms through the rest of the week until Sunday.

Mr. Frye came for me this morning, saying Mrs. Eddy wanted I should take the picture and go with him and finish it at her house. So I took it up. Almost instantly upon seeing the results of my efforts she disapproved of the pictures of the children. Soon with much emphasis she pointed out the particular figures that she did not like and would *"not have in the picture."* She pointed to the very ones I had in the picture on Thursday for her inspection which she then approved, but they had been "worked up" as artists phrase it, which made them show plainer.

She told me to go into the usual room over the library and take out all of the figures that showed anything more than the faces of the forms. She said she *"would not* have anything of this personality represented which was according to the old idea, as if heaven was a breeding place of personal forms as this world of belief is."

I went to work and pretty soon she came in and began to talk to me, more as if the need of doing so had increased to her sense after I had come out. Mrs. Eddy talked vehemently to me that I *"must* awake out of this sleep."

Said she, "You ought to be seeking every hour of the day to be standing in the strength of God that you may be doing something. I have told you over and over, but you don't pay the least attention to me, and the result is animal magnetism has its own way at the Concord publishing office and we get nothing done but worthless work." Then she went out.

Later, in fifteen or twenty minutes, she came again. She came forward to just behind me as if to look over my shoulder at the work I was doing. She did so naturally, bending forward and placing a hand lightly on each of my shoulders as I sat leaning forward to the work, as if to steady herself while bringing her eye near enough to see clearly the rather fine work of the picture. As she did this, she delicately gave me a shaking as if to arouse me, saying kindly but in a vehement undertone voice, "Arouse yourself! You *must* wake up!"

I got on well on the picture, making the changes she had directed, and the work progressed rapidly toward completion. She came in and watched me a while and said that she wanted I should promise her one thing. She said, "I want you to stay to lunch, and I want you to promise me that you will come every day and work and stay to lunch with me until you get these pictures done."

Later on the way to the Publishing Office I reflected that she certainly was right in regard to that picture. It *did* reflect personality, and it *was* immeasurably better as it was now, and not only more spiritual, but more original and effective and taking. The thought came that Jesus said truly, "By their fruits ye shall know them."

In the night I waked and the thought came to me that I might profitably sit up and watch for a while in order that I might realize more deeply the power of God to enable me to keep spiritually awake.

In about forty minutes I began to *realize* that *life is spiritual* and that its sense is separate from material sense and not really affected by it in one way or another. I also gained the sense that labor in God's vineyard is in having faith enough to combat the claims of personal mortal mind and in doing this, to learn that such labor was and forever *is* a labor *of joy* and not of burden or of heaviness of heart. I worked vigorously and resolutely in affirming the C.S. truth of being. It became plain that to keep awake spiritually here was the sure way to walk. Before the hour was up I felt I could *easily* give another hour or more, now that I felt that Christ had come to my consciousness.

TUESDAY, AUGUST 15, 1893

Today, early, I went up to Mrs. Eddy's. The second plate of "Christ-cure" which they had before made was worse than the first. I was too early, and I arranged to be called for at eleven A.M. by Mrs. Sargent with carriage. Mrs. Sargent talked with me profitably in the carriage on the way back to Mrs. Eddy's of

Original drawing for "The Way," also called "The Ascension"

other minds' influence, saying we had got to recognize this as an evil to be destroyed by treatment. Arriving at Pleasant View I found Mrs. Eddy liked the "Ascension" picture as now finished. After lunch I fixed some little things to complete it to suit Mrs. Eddy's thought, then took it down to the publishing house to be copied, waited, and treated [prayerfully] again. The first negative was splendid, the operator saying he was surprised himself at the result.

WEDNESDAY, AUGUST 16, 1893

Today, I went up to Mrs. Eddy's again with the proof from the printer of the text of the poem for Mrs. Eddy to correct. I took also the five most important sepia pictures, also all the proofs that were very good from half tone plates, for Mrs. Eddy to pass upon. She approved most of the plates and suggested some improvements in the originals which I proceeded to make while there, having my brushes with me.

THURSDAY, AUGUST 17, 1893

Soon after my arrival at Pleasant View Mrs. Eddy told me that she had called to see Mr. Pearson, the business manager of the publishing house here, and he at once admitted that the making of the plates was a failure.

I related the following to Mrs. Eddy just before luncheon time and she asked me to repeat it to others of her household at the lunch table if I would "please do so."

Being an artist as well as student of Christian Science, I

naturally feel a deep sense of beauty, even that which is truly described in our textbook, *Science and Health,* "Beauty is a thing of life, which dwells forever in the eternal Mind and reflects the charms of His goodness in expression, form, outline, and color."[24] But as I told Mrs. Eddy, I was deceived under the cover of her approval of my rough sketch of the design of the cherub forms into tolerating the thought that I was at liberty to think and express the personal sense in some degree at least when it related to the beauty of innocent nude cherub child forms required for this "Ascension" picture. Soon this personal sense began to so dominate my consciousness until, even in the self-satisfied sleep that it engendered, I became aware that I was giving too much attention to the merely external appearance of the forms and thus was violating the spiritual import of the picture. This awakened me to see the material thought I was tolerating. I at once turned about enough to attempt outward correction by erasures and the further execution in a more spiritual way, but without having the thought that my personal self-satisfied state of mind was what needed correction. To allow that "beauty unadorned is adorned the most," when applied to a material human form appearance, even though perfect and symmetrical outwardly, is to lose sight entirely of the real beauty, which is always spiritual, constituting a likeness of Truth and Love. Seeking earnestly to know this by looking to Spirit for the ability to realize it was the real cleansing that was needed. But this was left for Mrs. Eddy to initiate and carry out.

When she saw the picture, Mrs. Eddy vigorously pointed to the different figures that must come out, saying in the voice of indignant command, *"Take that out! and that! and that!"* each time singling out the figures where shoulders and arms were represented, which I had worked over with personal satisfaction. Some were figures that were there when she first had approved, but I had worked over them some seeking to perfect the beauty of their forms as it then appeared to me.

Mrs. Eddy was so sensitive to error's work, she was *feeling* it, although its outward form was not in evidence to corroborate it. Her spiritual sensitivity to mental states of consciousness whereby the measure of the personal and material in the thought of those with whom Mrs. Eddy is with is unmistakably manifest to her. This causes her at once to feel and know, that the ideal beauty of God's goodness is being violated. This material thought is *felt* as very offensive to her pure sense of Spirit, and therefore, as in my case, demanding the rebuke that cures it.

At the lunch table Mrs. Sargent and Mr. Frye listened attentively to my explanation. Mrs. Sargent thanked me kindly for what I had stated, saying that it contained a great lesson for her. Mrs. Eddy appeared greatly gratified both when I told it first to her and now at the table. She said, "that was the way it has been all through [my life]." She explained that her mother had brought her up to be very kind and considerate and peace-loving in her ways with others. It was not lack of self-control that made her so often appear unjust, or ungenerous, or unkind, or impatient, but the obedience to God which she dare not disregard. She referred to the life of Jesus, saying, "Could there have been anything more pungent or severe than his words against error, even toward his immediate disciples? 'Get thee behind me, Satan,' was his word to Peter—the strongest language he could have used." She referred to her great loneliness because people could not understand her.

Robert Lincoln's[25] family called previous to lunch while Mrs. Eddy was with me watching changes I was making on the picture, "Seeking and Finding." Mrs. Sargent was in the room at the time, and looking out of the window at the carriage waiting at the gate, and the figure advancing to the front door, she said, "Why, Mother! There is Jessie Lincoln." Then as she advanced to go down, she stopped and asked Mrs. Eddy, "Will you see them?" Mrs. Eddy replied simply, "No, not today." She had not paid much attention to Mrs. Sargent's remark that "There was Jessie Lincoln," except to leisurely turn her head and look out of the window and then back again to the work I was doing. When we afterwards were going down to lunch, she referred to this example of her equal regard for people in high station in life to those of humbler station, saying that was the way she had been all along.

While at work on the picture, I spoke of something which moved me to tears. Mrs. Eddy reached up her handkerchief (she was sitting just on one side, a little behind me and lower than I), and wiped them away tenderly and in silence.

While at lunch, I said, "Mrs. Eddy, you are fortunate in having such a good cook," for the cooking and preparation of the food was very excellent. Mrs. Eddy answered that it was so indeed, adding, "It is through Christian Science that this excellence has appeared, for before she applied the Principle of Christian Science to her work she was a poor cook," a statement Mrs. Sargent corroborated. Pretty soon "Martha,"[26] the cook, came in and Mrs. Eddy said to her: "Mr. Gilman was commending your cooking and I told him that you were a Christian Scientist in your cooking." "Yes," she cordially replied, "it is only by carrying Christian Science practice into my work that I have been able to do it well."

SATURDAY, AUGUST 19, 1893

Called upon Mrs. Eddy at 11 o'clock to leave the balance of the pictures. Mrs. Eddy came down to see me just as I was about to go. At this time I spoke again of the idea of the getting up of a group of photographs by Mr. Brown.[27] I had called this to her attention before on August 3rd when we were coming up from the boathouse, and now she still further endorsed the idea. She told me of two photos that a girl of sixteen had made of the place and the pond, Mr. Easton's daughter[28] of Boston. She wanted I should go up to the sitting room with her and she would get them and show me, which I did. While there I suggested that one of our views be one of her sitting room with herself sitting in her armchair and the chair in which she wrote *Science and Health,* in the view. She approved of the idea and then began to talk of the writing of *Science and Health.*

"I moved nine times while writing the book and that chair was the only furniture and about all I possessed. My writing desk was simply a piece of book cover cardboard. There was no good reason for my moving except the antagonism that was felt to the ideas, and to me for voicing them. In one case the woman of the house having ordered me to go, I got all ready to go, but I wanted to write a few paragraphs that I had in thought and went into the kitchen to do it. The woman tried to smoke or steam me out by throwing water on to the hot stove, thus making so much steam that she could not stay in the room. But I kept right on writing, paying no attention to it." The woman's husband was before this an infidel, but seeing how Mrs. Eddy bore these persecutions, he became a Christian.

One of Mrs. Eddy's near relatives, she said, offered to give her a beautiful residence and home by herself and a maintenance if she would give up her nonsense, as she called it. I replied that it was fortunate for us all that she did not give way to them.

> Pleasant View, Concord, N.H.
> August 22

Mr. Gilman
My dear friend
Call on me tomorrow immediately after 9 a.m. I want you to lithograph my pictures and want to talk to you about them.

> With high regard,
> Mother

THURSDAY, AUGUST 24, 1893

I saw Mr. Frye this morning as I was going to breakfast. I was ten or fifteen minutes earlier than usual for me and came across him with the carriage just at the crossing of one of the streets in the business portion of the town. The time was 6:20 A.M. I write of this because it seemed at the time as if it all had been perfectly provided so that when I had arrived at the crossing Mr. Frye had also. He immediately said without surprise at seeing me, "Good morning, get right in," turning the horse a little as suiting the action to the word. He carried me on down to my boarding place, saying it was as near home by that way as from where we started. Soon after getting into the carriage, he said he had a message for me from Mrs. Eddy to call up there at nine o'clock that morning. He said, "I reckoned I should see you somewhere along here."

Before nine o'clock it came on to storm heavily with strong wind from the southeast. Nevertheless, I went up, arriving a little before nine. I was ushered into the library as usual by Mrs. Sargent. After waiting a little, Mrs. Eddy called to me from the top of the stairs, saying in a pleasant voice, "Come up here to my sitting room," to which I responded at once, of course. She had a paper in her hand as she stood at the top of the stairway, as if she had just completed some business arrangements with Mr. Frye. She welcomed me with a cordial grasp of the hand.

She immediately afterward began to say, after seating herself and causing me to be seated, that there was a work ready to be done, and asked me if I was ready to do it. She said, "Now, Mr. Gilman, are you ready for the work God has for you to do?" I replied that I believed that I was according to my ability. Upon this she extended her hand and we clasped hands as if to solemnize a sacred compact. She continued, "I am going to trust that you are," at the same time handing me a check already made out for twenty dollars, saying, "You know how they have failed here at the publishing house to bring out these pictures. You see how malicious mind, or antagonism to Christian Science, is working to prevent this work from being brought out." I told her I had seen and had learned a lesson and should now know better how to intelligently combat it. "Oh, I guess you have," said she with a good deal of unction.

She continued, "It has been just so with the publication of *Science and Health* and *Introspection*.[29] The presses would *snap* or refuse to work, or the pressmen would be sick. Fifteen men were flat on their backs with sickness at one time and they could not go on with the work until we took up the work, healed the men and handled the difficulty mentally in Science. I know the source from which this comes. *It is theosophy.* That is the form the arch enemy takes now. They are concentrating all their energies against Christian Science, for they know it is their foe of all foes. I could tell you of things that have happened here in consequence that would startle you, but I won't frighten you. It works in the form of electricity, but it has no power."

The storm outside was now furious and the gale shook the casements and jarred the house, while the rain was driven violently against the windowpanes. I said, "The elements seem angry this morning."

"Do you see how it is?" said she with a knowing look, "but God will calm the storm." I told her I had been tempted by the thought that she would think me foolish to come up in such a storm, but that I was feeling in the mood to meet and master the storm as the type of the mental elements arrayed against me.

"Do you see how the animal magnetism is continually suggesting an opposite course to the right one?" she said. "But now to the work we have in hand. God has told me we must *hide the Child* and I want you to be ready to start for Gardner, Massachusetts, next Monday morning. I have arranged it with Benny. He will meet you there. I have had the pictures sent in a stout box to him by express. "Benny has promised that he will help you and you are to help the man who gets up the reproductions to do the work right. But you are not to tell him for whom the work is being done."

Then she said interrogatively, "Do you know how to keep a secret? They say a woman can't keep a secret, but I have learned how—let no one know that you *'have a secret'* and then you can keep it. You are not to tell any one here where you are going, but tell them you are going for a while to some town that you know you will pass through, so that you need not lie to them." I told her I should have to pass through the town of my father whom I should visit before my return, and to say I was going to visit my father would be accurate.[30] "That is just the thing," said she, "You are going home for a visit." Then she asked Mr. Frye to bring in the package she had had him prepare. Opening it, she took out two or three of the "half tone" pictures that had been printed from the plates of the publishing house here to use as samples of the size she wanted the new plates to be. At the bottom of these she had pinned mottoes from the Bible. On one of them she had quoted from Matthew 4:16, crediting it to Jesus. I said that I did not think that they were Jesus' words. "Don't you?" said she. "Whose words, then?" I told her I thought they were John the Baptist's words. She then began to look in the New Testament for the quotation, but not finding it at once, it was left for Mr. Frye to look in the concordance and find it. When it was found that the words were a quotation by Matthew from the prophet "Esaias," she laughed heartily.

While she was talking to me afterwards of the way to overcome the enemy successfully, she said good-naturedly that "if we could get Gilman out of way, we could get on all right. The great thing to do was to get rid of Gilman." She gave me her hand when I came to go and said, "God bless you. After this work comes out I have something to tell you, but I won't say anything more about it now."

MONDAY, AUGUST 28, 1893

When I arrived in Gardner, I opened this letter from Mrs. Eddy. She handed it to me before I left Concord with the instruction, "do not open this till your arrival."

August 25

My dear friend.

Be sure and have the pictures that I enclose a list of struck off first. When the proofs are correctly taken then send these 4 to me. Enclose them in a sealed package directed to me then put on another wrapping directed to J. M. Runnels, Opera House Block, Concord, N.H. And will request Mr. R. to send or bring them to me.[31] Please hand the enclosed to Dr. Eddy immediately on arriving or as soon as you get his address in Gardner.

And now may grace and peace and watchfulness and prayer be and abide with you.

Lovingly,
Mother

Pictures to be struck off first and sent to me:

Seeking and Finding
Healing the Sick
Unity
Knocking

TUESDAY, AUGUST 29, 1893

Gardner, Mass.

Dear Mother in Truth,

Mr. Carlton[32] is doing well in the work so far. He has made the preliminary negatives from the four that you have designated to be made first and they *are very excellent negatives*. The quality of the pictures depends the most upon these negatives being good, and they are good. The one "Seeking and Finding" he made this morning when the storm raged as if possessed of the evil one. He had to try twice and the last one he timed five times as long as usual on account of the storm darkness which continued nearly all the forenoon.

The glory of spiritual Being was revealed to me nearly all the way on the train from Concord here as much as I could receive and as never so fully before, for which I am indebted to you in your faithfulness to Truth. Shall I ever be able to repay such indebtedness? I never can I know. I like Mr. Carlton very much. He is not in the least self assertive or disposed to mind any business but his own, and he is fine and delicate in his sensibilities. He showed the Dr. and I about some of the pleasantest parts of the town last evening between five and six o'clock. He expects to have some good proofs of the four on Thursday perhaps in the forenoon. Possibly we can get them to you by Thursday night or Friday morning.

Gratefully and Truly Yours
James F. Gilman

P.S. I am afraid that five inches long will be a little too small for "Chaos" and Christmas Tree. I enclose some slips of paper that I have cut out with their size marked on them. Now, don't you think the 5½ inch long one and the 6 inch long one is small enough for the pictures which I have designated on their surfaces? Please let me know if you agree with me that the larger sizes are small enough.

Truly
J. F. G.

THURSDAY, AUGUST 31, 1893

Dear Mother,

The proofs of the four were forwarded by express tonight as you have directed, to Mr. R_____. The Dr. has written and put it in with the proofs. But I think it was forgotten to say anything of the titles and mottoes, or passages of scripture to go under the pictures. This will have to be done by the printer as the putting of them in right is not adapted to this form of printing that we are doing here in the making of the prints. I thought the absence of this on the proofs without explanation might perplex you. I think the proofs sent are good. Mr. Carlton says that as the men grow familiar with the requirements of the plates they improve in the quality of the prints they produce. It was so with Mr. Runnels' lot. They were better than the proofs submitted.

Very Truly Yours,
James F. Gilman

FRIDAY, SEPT. 1, 1893

I received the following from Mrs. Eddy in response to my letter of August 29:

Sept. 1, '93

Mr. Gilman
My dear friend,

All hail! He will hide thee till the storm has passed. Abiding in Truth and Love we are blessed; and the wrath of man shall praise Him. I like your *measures* just sent. Go on and as rapidly as possible with correctness.

Most thankfully
with tender regard.
M. B. G. Eddy.

Mrs. Eddy acknowledged receipt of the proofs in the following letter:

Pleasant View, Concord, N.H.
September [1, 1893]

My dear Friend

I am *satisfied*—Go right on. Rec'd your proofs this
P.M. Please send nothing through any mail that you
prefer not to have read. I see no need of your sending
the remaining proofs to me. You and my dear son can
pronounce on them. The *artist* knows his business.
This will facilitate your return, and the Dr. wants to
come back as well as you.

Lots of love to him.
Many thanks.
Affectionately,
M. B. G. Eddy

I shall start these on the Express Tomorrow, Sept. 2.
I have put my initials on those I fancy most. But they
all are done so finely it is hard to chose.

Tell darling Benny I want to write him but I have
no moments to spare for anything.

THURSDAY, SEPTEMBER 7, 1893

Returned tonight on the 5:40 train from Gardner with good
proofs from all the plates from the illustrations. Took a hack in
order to have my trunk carried to my room, and made ready at
once to go up to Mrs. Eddy's with the proofs. Upon starting at
6 o'clock it began to rain vigorously. Took the car to upper

Pleasant St. After leaving the car it rained heavily. Mrs. Eddy greeted me with a hearty welcome. Instead of asking to see the proofs that were in the package I carried, she handed me a book or pamphlet advertising half-tones, various kinds of type, &c. saying, "Here is a book showing specimens of half-tone which Mr. Frye has received. I thought you would be interested in that." I glanced at the publication a little and laid it aside saying, "But you want to see these proofs I have first," to which she assented. In seeing them she expressed hearty approval as each proof was brought to view, her expressions being all in the superlative. She called Mrs. Sargent to admire them with her, describing them as being "just like steel engravings," saying that generally she did not like Mrs. Sargent's profuseness of expression, but now she wanted to hear them.

Matters went this way until she asked me if there were any others but these out. I answered, "no" except that the Doctor had taken a set with him to Boston. This proved to be a spark to ignite an outburst of indignation against the Doctor. Her first word was to Mrs. Sargent. "There, Laura, did I not tell you so this morning. I knew there was something wrong with the Doctor. Did you ever see anything like it; the way that boy disobeys me? To think that after I had expressly told him not to do this very thing, he should go and do it. Oh! Oh! I will telegraph him now, and will you take the telegram down, Mr. Gilman?"[33]

That night I got a hackman to take up the trunk of pictures from the railroad station, I going up with it. When I was at Pleasant View, Mrs. Sargent handed me a letter from Mrs. Eddy. She wrote,

Sept. 7

Confidential

My dear friend,

What a history is mine! I am always betrayed. No matter how true I am to others they can always be made false to me.

Now I own these pictures and they have cost me dear. I hereby request you to return to me every copy of them that you have in your possession, and the one that has the indefinite serpent on it which you mentioned. Also if you regard my feelings at all I ask as a special favor that you *name* to *no one* except Mr. Runnels, what you have been doing. Keep it utterly *still*, don't let it get into the minds of others. The Dr.'s cruel indifference to my expressed and emphasized desire has prevented me carrying out my plans. I shall not send my book to Chicago and shall finish my book when God tells me to. But shall wait on Him. He alone can I trust. *Man* works against us both.

With kind regards

M B G Eddy

MONDAY, SEPTEMBER 11, 1893

Went up to Mrs. Eddy's immediately after dinner.

She had a fresh new look to me which made me say, "You look like an entirely new personage today." It seemed a droll remark to make, but it was a spontaneous expression. She thought so, for an instant perhaps, and then she began to say that last night she had come to revelations that had exceeded anything she had had before, in which she saw plainly that all things were put under her feet and the love of God was so manifest, it exceeded anything she could describe. "All things were dissolved in it; all sense of evil, all antagonism; nothing was left but the sea of God's immeasurable Love." I felt awed and as if a word in response from me would be sacrilege.

She continued: "I shall not go to Chicago," and referred to Mr. Kimball[34] there as having carried out her work gloriously and as a faithful and true student. The World's Fair she thought "would prove to be a means of great dissemination of Christian Science, but I shall not be there. It is better to be here with God."

Soon she said, "I forgot I am expecting visitors[35] here soon and I must not delay." I told her my errand and she assented to the taking of pictures of her sitting room, but said she would not be in it. I expressed sorrow at this, saying, "We need you in the room or it will look empty." But she said, "No, I am tired of the caricatures that they always get of my expression. But you can make my portrait. I am going to have you make it when I get time and I will help you, but not now." "But," I said, "I was going to have you looking down in this picture and wasn't going to try to get your expression of face." I suppose I looked so sorrowful that she felt compassion, for she replied, "Well, to please you I will," her face lighting with a smile as she said it.

As my face showed much feeling I suppose, she looking up at me (she had been standing at the door ready to go) and said compassionately, "You are a good boy, only you are disobedient. I know," she replied to my look of doubt, "You are unintentionally so."

TUESDAY, SEPTEMBER 12, 1893

Went up to Pleasant View with Mr. Brown as per appointment at 9:30 a.m. to take negatives. We found Mrs. Eddy dressed in the fine white silk dress that was a gift from her students.

Everything being in readiness, she reading one of her student's letters, we exposed the plate and returned to town. Mr. Brown immediately developed the negative which appeared tolerable with the exception of her feet which were not posed gracefully. I went up and showed the proof in the afternoon and it was not liked by Mrs. Eddy, who said she should not ever sit for another one. I told her I thought we could remedy the defects of this plate in another, and finally after much urging by Mrs. Sargent and myself, she consented to sit for just one more and that was all. I went back to Mr. Brown's much pleased at this. We made great plans for being sure of getting a good one the next time, and then I returned to my room to work.

I had not been there more than an hour before Mr. Frye rang and said Mrs. Eddy wanted I should bring up that negative in the morning when I came up, to which I assented. He went away, but came back in two or three minutes telling me that Mrs. Eddy wanted to see me at the carriage. Arriving there, she asked me to get into the carriage with her and then said she wanted to go up and have me get her the negative then. As soon as we started, she began to say that she shouldn't have another negative taken in the morning as had been arranged. "Now," she said, "I won't hear a word of remonstrance. I have listened too much to you already. It is taking my thought and attention from God's work and God has told me that I must put a stop to this."

MONDAY, SEPTEMBER 18, 1893

I went up to Mrs. Eddy's this morning at 9 o'clock.

"Now, Mr. Gilman, I want you to make a success of this picture or series of pictures of the place which I have given you the right to make," she said. "This place and spot where 'Mother' has lived will be of growing and sacred interest as Christian Science becomes disseminated.[36] But, oh, I want you should do it in such a way that God and Christian Science shall be glorified and the Cause advanced for it *is* a way of salvation, is it not? If only you could know how I have struggled and wrestled to overcome this wave of hatred and resistance to Truth, and now I have won the way to Love's victory of peace and calm.

"In the case of the negative of me in my room I hated to destroy it, but I felt irresistibly impelled by God that I must do it, and in obeying, I felt I had broken their idols." I told her that I had felt spiritually that my idols were being broken since she had gotten this negative. I was thankful she was so faithful and true to God, for it has liberated me from bondage that was holding me through them which I can now see. She continued, "Yes, that is it."

She said if we (the Doctor and I) could only know how much she labored to have us realize the Truth spiritually. She said it was such a grievous sin to be talking scientifically all the time and not *realizing* the Truth. She said she had wrestled with the Spirit for us in a degree no one could know and could only take us to God and leave us there, trusting to His omnipotent grace. She expressed this with great feeling and with an upward, far-away look in her face that I cannot accurately describe.

SATURDAY, SEPTEMBER 23, 1893

This morning was favorable to taking the balance of the outside views, so Mr. Brown and I went out about 9 o'clock. The morning had been foggy, but just after eight it cleared. When we arrived, the house was in splendid light for a picture, but clouds in the west were rising and threatened to shade the house soon if we did not hasten. Preparing the camera in place for the best view of the house, we saw that a white banner, which was flying from its support projecting out from the tower balustrade, looked badly and would be hard in the photograph to make out. Its shape and white color made it look some like some garment of linen wear which appeared to be hanging to dry on the balustrade.

Engrossed in the idea of getting a good picture, such as would honor the place, I failed to think that possibly the banner, which she had before showed me at a previous time as a gift from one of her students, was hung out for some other purpose than that of having it in the picture. I thought it was there to be in the picture, so I thought it all important that it be where it would show plain and good. I rang at the door, telling Mrs. Sargent how it was, asking her to speak to Mrs. Eddy about it and to ask her to move it about six feet the other way. So Mrs. Eddy went out and pushed it out a little, as much as she could owing to the fastenings. But it appeared to me that that did not help it any, and full of haste, lest the rising clouds shade the house, I told her it would not show good there. She appeared unwilling to move it and asked me if another view of the house would not show it better. I told her yes, but that then the house would not look as well.

I asked if I might not come up and fix it where it would look all right. She replied reluctantly, "Yes, if you think you can fix it better." So I rushed up the front stairs and Mrs. Sargent came out from Mrs. Eddy's room and told me to go through Mr. Frye's room from which a door opened on to the south verandah. Mrs. Eddy was out there when I arrived and I found that the banner staff was fastened by many strings to the balustrade on either side, and also to a heavy flower pot with earth and a small century plant in it. Mrs. Eddy did not seem pleased at the idea of my coming up and appeared to be trying to untie the strings which were attached to keep the banner from being blown about by the wind. I told her I would take care of it. "Well, you look out you do not injure that plant," she said, and then retired into her sitting room, drawing down the curtains almost as soon as she went in. But I was so full of self-will that these hints were insufficient to arrest my headlong way. I could see no good in anything beside the getting of this picture, forgetting entirely that the banner was but a slight feature in the picture, and that tender considerateness was of far more value than any picture, however good.

I had much work in getting the strings untied, and the banner with the flower pot moved, and I came near cutting one of the leaves of the century plant off with the string. I had now to ask that Mrs. Eddy raise her curtains while the picture was being made, which she did at once. In going down to go out, I saw Mrs. Sargent who regretted that I had to move the banner as "Mother had been at much pains to put it where it was and would want it put back there again when the picture had been made." She said that "it had been put out in honor of the triumph of Christian Science at Chicago at the Religious Congress. The Christian Science address had been read the day before and highly commended by leading officials there as one of the most notable contributions to the success of the Parliament of Religions." Upon putting it back in place, which I did immediately, the exposure being made, as I was going in to go upstairs, I met Mrs. Eddy coming out dressed for a walk, with her parasol. Her steps were directed toward the boathouse and she said to me reproachfully, "You have driven me away from my devotions, and I must go where I can be alone."

SUNDAY, SEPTEMBER 24, 1893

I wrote to Mrs. Eddy.

> Dear Patient Mother:
> I have been in sorrow and heaviness since yesterday because I give place to so much of self will that spiritual love, joy, and considerateness is put aside from present consciousness and therefore dishonored and unreflected. This adds needlessly to your already awful burdens of which I really know nothing. The question, "What shall I do to be saved?" has become to me a living, vital, terrible question. The more I think I am able to answer this question, and strive accordingly to put it into practice, the further away from the kingdom of God I plainly

appear to be drifting. I see that my supposed attainments as an artist and as a Christian are nothing but self-love and self-will and self-justification, in subtle forms, more dangerous than open bald manifestations of the same in avowed worldliness. The only artist is the one who *loves* and adores Truth first of all, and last of all. This will keep the ruthless hand still, and open eyes that are blind to everything but their own fond beliefs. A spark of the divine Love and Truth has now and then in these later weeks appeared to my view in response to your faithfulness, no doubt, giving me the desire that these sparks of divinity shall be fanned into a burning flame in my realization, daily, as the valuable and precious sense of Life only that is Real for which I stoutly resolved to be ready, always, to sacrifice self; and the "headlong self-will" of yesterday seems to be the result. But it isn't, is it, Thou Loved One of God? Hidden away somewhere is reason for hope and knowledge that your labor is not in vain.

> Sincerely your would-be
> disciple,
> James F. Gilman

In the afternoon, after walking to Rattlesnake Hill at West Concord to see the quarries, and dwelling upon my case and seeking humility, I gained some sense of God's presence as the salvation from which I had been drifting. On this day I gained a still clearer view of what self-will was, and self-love, and self-justification, and that I was possessed of them all in unusual degree. And I saw it to be actually so. This appears to me a very valuable lesson. Once before I had gained a perception that I was self-willed and saw that it was a somewhat different quality than I had supposed it to be. I had not been conceiving that a *benevolently* inclined person could, in *that,* be self-willed. And now I saw plainly the error of this and how very self-willed I am in nearly all that I do. I even begin to suspect that in the writing of this I may be so, as I realize a sense of urgency to get it done that I may retire to rest and so I now stop.

MONDAY, SEPTEMBER 25, 1893

Received a very dear letter from Mrs. Eddy today in response to the one I had written her last evening. The letter she wrote was one of motherly encouragement, as follows:

> Pleasant View, Concord, N.H.
> September 25, [1893]
>
> Dear Seeker
> Be of good cheer. All thy shortcomings are forgiven for that day. I had a glorious season with God. You are not only seeking but gaining slowly. Seeing your errors always presages their destruction and like a fever raging before it ceases—the error looks bigger even when becoming less.
> With best wishes, and wishes that you had had my pictures on the proper paper,
> I am Mother,
> M. B. G. E.

Concord, N.H.
September 27, 1893

Dear Mother,

Your dear letter was duly received, but the Light of your Truthful thought had come to me before it and I was gratefully rejoicing in the sense of the marvelous Goodness of God to me, who am so unworthy of the favors He is pouring upon me. I have been enabled to *see* that I am full of self-love and self-will; and, as you have so truly stated somewhere, it is more than one-half the battle to *see* the error we would uncover and thus destroy. It seems to me I also am beginning to perceive something of the glory of the Divine Idea as manifested in thy faithfulness, patience, and compassion which is the Love of the Divine One made manifest in this our fortunate day and age. I believe I see also that the varying circumstances of this life are of value and moment, only as they are made to serve as occasions for the manifestations and illustrations of the beauty, reality and completeness of the *spiritual* sense of being.

Oh may I steadily keep in view what I am graciously being taught. That material circumstances must find only *secondary* place in my thought, that the first place may be honored by the love of Truth's glorious presence, in the consciousness that it includes all Good.

Very Truly and gratefully
James F. Gilman

There is another package from Gardner, at Mr. Runnels' store.

THURSDAY, OCTOBER 5, 1893

Mrs. Eddy sent for me today to bring my paper and sketching materials and come and do some sketching. I rode up with the young man who brought me word. (It was after two o'clock when he finally found me) and we overtook Mrs. Eddy's carriage as she was returning from her daily drive. She rode earlier than usual today. Just as we passed the carriage, the man I was riding with came to his destination, and upon getting out, Mrs. Eddy motioned me to get in and ride the rest of the way in her carriage.

She immediately began describing a view from her verandah as it appeared at lunch time in a peculiar light. She said the view surpassed all description. She had sent for me that I might see and sketch it, but the light had changed now. When we arrived at the house, she asked me upstairs and went with me out on the verandah, saying, "Oh! I wish you could have seen it. The distance looked as clear as if right at hand and the light streaming down from the clouds looked like the rays in the 'Christmas morn' illustration." Pretty soon she began talking of the Chicago presentation of Christian Science. After expressing much joy, and how Joseph Cook[37] was represented as looking in the papers after hearing the presentation of her address before the Religious Parliament, she said that Joseph Cook said to someone that she, Mrs. Eddy, was "'a charlatan and had been driven out of Boston.' A Christian Science lady overhearing it turned indignantly and told him that *that was a lie.* 'Then I am a liar,' says Joseph. 'I repeat it,' says the lady.'" Changing her

"View Looking Southward from the Verandah"

"The Pond (Evening)"
In this drawing of Pleasant View, the man
in the boat is probably James F. Gilman.

tone of exultation to sadness, Mrs. Eddy said that "it was an awful thing that the Christian Scientists allowed themselves to be betrayed into giving her address to the papers." She said, "It was a crime." I said, "Doubtless the reporters took it down verbatim as it was delivered." She said, "No, they gave it to the reporters." She now excused herself, saying she was sorry to have troubled me to come up for nought, the glory of the landscape scene having passed away.[38]

SUNDAY, OCTOBER 15, 1893

Thursday I went up to sketch from Mrs. Eddy's south verandah the view in the direction of the scene she had been so enraptured by on the day I was last there. She was walking down the path to the boathouse with her parasol in the bright sunlight when I arrived at the house. I disliked to go up and go to sketching from there without Mrs. Eddy being consulted or informed of the fact. Mr. Frye agreed with me it would perhaps be better to see her first. As I approached the boathouse, I heard singing, which I knew must be Mrs. Eddy. She sang a familiar hymn. There appeared no way but to stop and wait out of sight until she ceased singing.

She sang very expressively and the cadence of her voice and the words as in this song ran in my mind more or less all the time until today. When she ceased I appeared in the doorway and she turned and gave me a welcome smile and extended her hand. "Wasn't it strange," she said, "that I should look up and find you waiting at the door at this time." After asking me how I got on, she asked me to sit and soon began talking of the Chicago

matter and told me "the old story of the parting of Christ's gar-
ments among them (his enemies) was being repeated again
today." She then quoted some Scriptural prophecy of Revelation
and said it was being fulfilled today. She said many things which
I cannot write of much, partly because I did not understand fully
the meaning of what she was saying. Perhaps I ought to have had
the presence of mind to have excused myself after seeing her a
minute or two that I might not disturb her in her retirement.
One thing she emphasized in what she said, and that was that the
ethics of Christian Science raises people to a higher plane of
action in which all is mental instead of material. In this plane of
life, to steal is to take mental things that do not belong to us; and
to kill is to hate our neighbor; and so on through the Decalogue.
In this realm there is as yet no laws to restrain as there is in the
physical world, except the restraint of self-defense through under-
standing of Truth and the nothingness of error and sin.

WEDNESDAY, OCTOBER 25, 1893

It came to me this morning from the suggestion of a dream
what *obedience* really is. Obedience is not to look to matter for
a single thing, but to God for everything. To do less is to imply
that there is lack in God, in the proportion of our looking to
matter for the fulfillment of our desires. In this light I see the
import of Mrs. Eddy's repeated chiding of me for being so dis-
obedient. I see I have been disobedient nearly all the time,
without indeed consciously knowing it. To try to compass the
execution of a picture in mortal strength, is to look away from
God as the only source, and so to be disobedient.

I am greatly rejoicing in the perception of this truth, which began with the light that came last Sunday evening in my walk around a few streets west of the Post Office. In this walk I was feeling pointedly the unsatisfactoriness of life because of my inability to escape from mortal motives that would not down permanently, but like mosquitoes or flies that get away for the moment, continually return to torment as soon as the driving away process ceases.

During the day on Sunday, I had walked on the "Plains" (east of Concord). The day was beautiful outwardly and many suggestions of beauty were presented, awaking my sense of nature as inherently lovable and real power of expressing it in pastel painting. My yearnings were partly expressed in the following verse written while on the "Plains":

> Oh, that I might live the holy life
> Apart from sin and free from death,
> In which is stilled all mortal strife
> And Love transforms this empty earth
> To Heaven.

In the evening I thought I would walk a little. Perhaps it would awaken some liberating thought. As I walked, I was troubled by the glaring materiality of the electric lights. They spoiled the moonlight which was more spiritual, more in accord with the true sense of Life which I had understood from early life intuitively. This intuitive perception of the really beautiful in nature was the perception of the poetry of Life which was continually being spoiled by the materialities of the age which, like the electric lights and cars, and all other modern inventions, was allowed to be crowded in to interfere with the really good on every hand.

This was the flow of mortal belief, when the better thought came that this view of my intuitive perception as being spiritual and superior to the general thought was nothing but a more subtle form of materiality—self-love. Good was not interfered with really, and could not be, by electric lights or any other form of expressed materiality said this voice of Truth. I could just as deeply realize the poetry and complete goodness of God in one material light as another, if I saw God as everywhere. Good was spiritual only and was not touched by matter and could not be. Immediately I was immersed in Light from God's throne of Truth and purity and the electric lights looked as good and poetic as the moonlight, because I now saw *goodness everywhere* for God was everywhere to my sense. I saw also that to understand God in this way was to have *everything* that could be desired.

I was free to love this idea of Truth and to give my whole time to motives that were born of this idea of Truth, in which I should rejoice alone in opportunities for demonstrating it. That was the infinite all of being that Life expresses. Such opportunities were on every hand whatever I should do outwardly, and nothing could keep me from improving them. Thus I saw that God was *really* Life—all Life.

Later, as I was meditating upon this, after I had been reading in *Science and Health,* it came to me that these visions of living Truth that came to me with the force of spiritual revelation, and which I have been supposing were my original thoughts, were already expressed in an almost numberless variety of forms in the Bible, and more definitely and plainly in our great textbook—

Science and Health with Key to the Scriptures by Mrs. Eddy. Now it has begun to dawn upon me that these fresh, vivid impressions of the living truth of God are the result of Mrs. Eddy's thought and teaching, under whose loving guidance and direction I am now seeking to find my true way of life as a willing follower of her high spiritual revealings.

> Pleasant View, Concord, N.H.
> [November] 28

Dear friend

Please call on me. I have a bit of plan to lay before you and want you to come [at] your earliest opportunity at my [house] after receipt of this.

> Very truly,
> Mary B G Eddy

TUESDAY, NOVEMBER 28, 1893

I received a letter from Mrs. Eddy requesting me to call upon her at my earliest opportunity at her house. In her letter was enclosed her card with her hours written in pencil in the lower left-hand corner: "10 to 11 A.M. — 4:30 to 6 P.M." She wrote, "I have a bit of plan to lay before you." I went up about 4:45. She received me very cordially, saying laughingly as she took my hand, "I suppose you are quite well today." She wanted to see me about making her portrait.

"Now you are not to let any one know that you are making

this. Can you keep it, do you think? I want this should be between you and [me] and God. Don't even let any one in the house here know. I have seen that you are very sensitive to other people's thought. Why! I have seen Mr. Frye just go and speak to you after I had left an impression in your thought to be carried out in your picture and just that would be enough to efface my impression." In speaking of the making of the portrait, she referred to the one in the *New American Biographical Encyclopedia,* asking me if I had seen it. On learning that I had not, she said I must. So she called to Mrs. Sargent to get it. She said the artist *tried* to get the portrait—was very anxious to— "but you see what they have got there," showing me the book with picture. She told me she would like me to read the sketch so that I would get a good and clear impression from that in my thought, and she would leave me to that while she attended to something else.

After I had just about read it, I heard her talking in the dining room with Mrs. Sargent concerning something that had just arrived. Mrs. Sargent exclaimed, "Oh, isn't that just lovely?" After a little Mrs. Eddy opened the library door a little cautiously, asking me if I had finished reading the sketch. I replied that I had and she came in bringing a book, saying, "I have just received a copy of my illustrated poem." It was *Christ and Christmas.*

Taking a seat beside me, she was all animation to show it to me and enjoy with me this first appearance of the poem and all complete which we had labored on so much during the past summer. She seemed like a young lady as she sat near me in order to look over with me and point out the different styles of type and other features connected with its makeup at the printer's and binder's, which were new to me of course. She made me look at the covers, both front and back, and then inside the covers at the lining before proceeding to look inside the book. It was at this period of showing me the get up of the book that the leaf before the "Finis" that ends the printed matter of the poem, was brought to my view, revealing to me in the center of the leaf, alone, these words:

Rev. M. B. G. Eddy
and
Mr. J. F. Gilman
Artists[39]

This was unexpected to me, and far more than compensated the disappointment I had felt when Mrs. Eddy requested me, at the time of the first efforts to get good reproductions of the originals, not to have my name or initials on any of the illustrations as is common with artists to sign their pictures.

After looking it through, during which I read each verse of the poem as we came to it, she said, "Tea is ready, so we will attend to it." As she passed into the dining-room, she said to Mr. Frye, "The word 'versus' in 'Truth *versus* Error' should have been in italics because it is a Latin word. I see they haven't got it so in the book. Now, why *couldn't* this book have been gotten out without this mistake?" Mr. Frye said, "That should have been corrected in the proof." Mrs. Eddy said, "It was; I underlined the word, indicating that it should be in italics. Now, I want you to go right down in the morning and have that rectified." Mr. Frye said the books were all printed now. "Well, you can have it corrected for the next edition anyway."

At the tea table it was very pleasant, and I felt much at ease. After tea, she passed with me into the library and began to give me some kind admonition as to making the portrait, saying she wanted it for *Science and Health* and all her publications. This, however, she said at the first, when I came. When talking about my making the portrait, she also meant that I was to have the publishing of the portrait and the profit from so doing as my recompense for making the portrait. This she referred to again now, saying she often felt sad when thinking of me so lonely and destitute. "And now," she said, "I want you should get something out of this. You don't look out for your interests enough in this way. Yes, I know we must seek the kingdom of God and His righteousness first, but then we are not to refuse what he puts into our hands, for 'all these things will then be added unto you,' Jesus said." I had told her I wanted to make a good portrait without any regard to the material income, from which she seemed to assume that I was ready to *refuse* to take any recompense, which was not my thought. She said money used to flow into her hands the later years of the college teaching in such quantities that she knew scarcely what to do with it. But it came into her thought as from God, "to put it by for a rainy day or for future use." After this kindly admonition, she excused herself with a parting clasp of the hand and a "good-bye." I came away, she having previously had all of her photographs brought down, giving me such as would be of use to me that I had no copies of already.

Pleasant View, Concord, N.H.
Dec. 4 [1893]

Dear friend

My students like to see my hair in waves rather than curls.
My photos that you have are thus and you can imitate them.

I think you will succeed. You made the face of Jesus so excel-
lent in "Christian Unity." Of the face you now depict as
expressing the life that is parting with, looking away from, the
vanities of earth and beholding in part the secrets of Heaven.

When next you call will have a little book to give you.

Mother

Concord, Dec. 4, '93

Rev. Mary Baker G. Eddy
Dear Mother—

Your suggestion of what I should seek in this portrait is just
in line with my thought and the design of the work so far. I am
feeling that great things must be accomplished in this portrait
of "Mother", and that they will be, for I feel that God is pres-
ent, inspiring me with the perception of the beautiful images
of spiritual nature that are so appropriate and fitting in this
picture. It ought to be a picture that shall be a spiritual conso-
lation to look at to anyone. I should despair of success if I did
not feel that my work is simply to go ahead directly toward the
high mark, on general principles which I have learned in prac-
tice to know to silence self and fear, in the confidence that the
Real One will somehow do the important parts of the work
when self don't know it. My ideal is ever before me, but it is

vague, and, yet, *almost* defined so that I feel that I can find it with my brush if I work patiently for it, which I am freely willing to do.

What I feel that is wanted is the expression of "meekness and might," youthfulness and years, joy and delicacy and yearning and intelligence and faith, all in one—in short—*Love* divine expressed as Mother, who never grows old any more than Spirit does. The Christian graces are eminently *childlike* and it lately occurs to me that they give a youthful look to any face from which they are reflected, and that is the impression of you left with me when I was with you last. I am making two pictures, so that when I have gone as far as I dare to, lest I injure or spoil what I have done, I turn to the other until I have surpassed the first when I turn to that again. This helps destroy fear because it keeps my best safe, you see.

Yours Obediently
James F. Gilman

I think what I am doing will occupy me all of this week before I shall feel the need of seeing you in order to get your impressions but perhaps I shall be ready sooner. If I am I will write. If you desire to see me on Friday or Saturday will you write? telling me when to come. I do not expect I shall be fully satisfied with what I shall have then for you to see, but rather great expectation of gain from seeing you. I am sure that I have good foundations in design of pose and other things for the great picture I look for.

Yours truly,
James F. Gilman

Pleasant View, Concord, N.H.
Dec. 6

Dear friend

Your letter is the breathings of an artist after God. Oh may
the aspiration be fulfilled and you be satisfied with His likeness.

Cannot see you before next week, a dress maker keeps me
from heaven this week. Wish it was thoroughly in my heart that
even dress fitting could not cast it out.

As ever most truly,
Mary B G Eddy

Pleasant View, Concord, N.H.
Dec. 8

Dear friend

I have a request from God, it is this. Stop thinking of our
work—on my picture. Put it *all out of mind* and work on some-
thing else—until I tell you to begin again.

Most truly,
M B G Eddy

FRIDAY, DECEMBER 8, 1893

Received a letter from Mrs. Eddy this morning making request
from God to me to discontinue the work upon her portrait
until she should tell me to begin again. I had gotten it nicely
along, as it seemed to me, to where I could surely finish it in a

couple of days. I have given up all thought of it, putting it out of mind, as she requested.

SUNDAY, DECEMBER 17, 1893

It becomes plainer and more manifest each hour that I have succeeded through God's grace in demonstrating the supremacy of Spirit in my efforts of the past week which culminated in my efforts in canvassing yesterday in a good measure of confidence that somehow God's provision for me would appear. Last evening Mr. Walker expressed a desire for what I might be able to do for him. He was a little shy of expressing to me outright as if a little ashamed of wanting such feminine or poetic things as pictures other than mechanical ones. But when he saw I did not urge the matter upon him, he came back from departing from the store of Mr. Runnels', which was where I saw him, and began to praise my large picture of Concord. Gradually it began to appear that he wanted I should do some work for him of scenery that he liked. He supposed I could not do it in the winter, until I told him I could and should be very glad to do some such work for him if I could at this time. Upon which he arranged to have me come to his house tomorrow, Monday morning, before nine, and he would take me with him to show me. I have written this in detail because of the peculiar interest it has for me as a part of God's manifestation of supply which I have been looking for in faith to appear in some way. I feel sure if I had not been possessed of this spirit of faith at the time I met Mr. Walker at the store, that I should in the ordinary material anxiety for work, have shown it in some way that would have worked against my success. As it was, I left the matter all with God without fear or anxiety, and God did the work for me by making me appear attractive to the man.

Today I received a letter from Mr. Carlton of Gardner and in a postscript on the back side of his letter, which escaped my attention until just now, he expressed a desire that I should do two or three pictures for him that he might put photogravure copies of them upon the market by and by. Thus the glorious Truth becomes demonstrated that "God is a very present help in trouble," as the Bible teaches, and Christian Science makes clear.

TUESDAY, DECEMBER 19, 1893

Go up to Mrs. Eddy's to lunch today at noon in response to a letter received yesterday inviting me with the promise that she had "a laugh in store for you if nothing better." Arriving, Mrs. Eddy appeared at the top of the stairway with a written letter in her hand before Mrs. Sargent completed the taking charge of my things. She looked down the stairway to me with a welcome smile and greeting, immediately coming down. After her usual greeting by handclasp, she at once began to talk about the letters she had received concerning the Christmas book and the criticisms, mostly favorable, the unfavorable ones coming from New York. She then read me portions of a letter she had in hand from Miss Annie Dodge[40] of Boston who Mrs. Eddy said she valued greatly as an art critic because she had studied art in Europe a long time under the greatest advantages, having abundance of wealth. The letter was discriminatingly critical and highly commendatory of the illustrations, even comparing them in many respects favorably with the old masters of painting, especially the head and figure of Christ. The New York critics had written that one objection to the "Ascension" picture was that the scene was located in Concord, New Hampshire (doubtless owing to the New Hampshire appearance of the trees). I acknowledged to her that I myself had recently thought of that, having had more time to consider it. "But," I said after a little, "I do not know as we need to go back to Jesus' day in Palestine to represent this thought." To this she quickly agreed, and having been called to lunch some minutes before, she arose, saying to me, "Lunch is ready." She extended her hand and took mine and led me like a child into the dining-room to the table. She resumed her talking about adverse criticism, new thoughts occurring to her which she expressed in much gleefulness, saying she should write directly to the *Journal* and have added her later thoughts to the article she already had prepared. It was late in the month, but she should ask Judge Hanna to delay the *Journal,* and she believed he would. The substance of her fresh thought that she wanted added was that Christian Science was a modern thought and was appropriately expressed in modern surroundings. "There is too much looking backward two thousand years. They will find," she said, "that there is a *Way* here in Concord as well as in Palestine."

Mrs. Eddy was in a gay mood today, and most everything turned to laughter. Finally she said, "What would people think, could they see and hear our freedom of expression here at the table." Mrs. Sargent said, "I don't believe people generally who did not understand Science would know what to make of it."

Mrs. Eddy referred to the dinner talks of the time of Dr. Samuel Johnson. She related that at one time when John Sylvester was present and the requirement was that a couplet was to be thought of on the spot and expressed at once, something appropriate and witty, John Sylvester made one something like this, she said, as near as I can remember:

> Today, I, John Sylvester,
> Met your wife and kissed her.

Dr. Johnson responded something like this:

> My name is Johnson,
> Today I hugged your wife.

Sylvester says, "Why, there is no poetry in that." "No," says Johnson, "but there is truth in it." And Mrs. Eddy added: "That is where the saying originated: 'There is more truth than poetry' in a thing." Mrs. Eddy is very apt at quoting poetic lines from many different authors. Very often she hesitates after beginning to quote and looking upward and away, she will say, "How is it that that runs," and then promptly she will think of it, and finally get it all right.

After lunch she asked me, when she had taken a seat in the library, if I had done anything on her portrait recently. I answered, "No, not since I received your letter asking me not to work upon it." She said, "I do not know why I was impelled to request you not to work upon it." I said, "I have felt no doubt but it would be for the best, and now I *know* it was. I would not for anything exchange the experience I have had in consequence of that." Mrs. Eddy replied, "That came from obedience. You are much better in that than you have been. Oh, you don't know how I have worked to get you out of the disobedient condition. Why, I have raised the dead with less effort.

"Well now," she said, "I think it will be best now to go on with the portrait. They are writing me from the east and west to have a good picture made.

I told her I was beginning to see the importance of obedience and I saw by her recent article on "Obedience"[41] in *The Christian Science Journal,* that she was working of late with all the Scientists to get them to be obedient. "Yes," she said, "that is what I am doing."

In speaking of obedience, she referred to Mr. Nixon[42] as embodying a general feeling of unwillingness to obey her implicitly, as a little child. She represented him in this as being in the attitude of mind to feel it beneath him to obey her because she was a woman. "He would declare himself ready to obey God in whatever He might require of him, but to obey a woman, bah!" Continuing, she said, "We understand God and are ready to obey Him only so far as we understand and are ready to obey His highest representative in mortal life. Our love for God and consequent willingness to obey Him is never greater than our love for and willingness to obey His highest demonstrator."

She gave me at the lunch table an invitation to dinner on Christmas day. She referred to it by saying, "While I think of it I will say now, I want you to come and take dinner with us on Christmas—that is, what we call lunch."

MONDAY, DECEMBER 25, 1893

I went up to Mrs. Eddy's about twelve o'clock. Arriving, I found Doctor Foster Eddy there from Boston, who came into the library and welcomed me. Soon Mrs. Eddy came down. After greeting me, she began to repeat from Longfellow a couplet concerning Christmas that was very sweet. Soon lunch was ready, for she calls the twelve o'clock meal "lunch," and she led the way taking the Doctor by the hand as she did me the week before.

Mrs. Eddy noticed a large glass vase of flowers from which was hanging a card with the words, "Christ makes us free." Asking the Doctor from whom it came, he replied that "Mrs. Weller[43] who was down to the city at Mrs. Otis', from Boston, sent it up." Mrs. Eddy at this gave expression to indignation because of what our materialistic laws and modern thought allowed in the persecution, that Mrs. Weller had suffered on account of Christian Science. She explained to me that Mrs. Weller had lived in Littleton, New Hampshire, and that her husband had been granted a divorce from her on the ground that she made him sick by her practice of Christian Science.

In the course of the meal she referred to Milton as being blind, and Mrs. Sargent referred to some other noted man as being deformed in some way. Mrs. Eddy remarked how often it was that the great and noted of the world were subject to some grievous defect or deficiency. I replied after a little that there was one marked exception to what seemed to be the general rule, and that was in the example of George Washington. To this she assented and said there was one incident in his history which greatly impressed her and that was when they were thinking of making him king after the war, before the present form of government had been established.

Washington refused to be considered in that way and told them decisively that if ever they undertook such a thing he should leave the country or something to that effect. They had met together for some important purpose when this was being expressed, and Washington was asked to read something and he could not read it until his glasses could be produced. Waiting for this, he exclaimed, "Gentlemen, I have grown blind in your service!" as if he would reproach them in that having served them so long and so faithfully, they should now want to go contrary to his principles and wishes so much as to seriously think of making him king.

The conversation turned upon Mrs. Weller again. Mrs. Eddy asked the Doctor why he did not ask Mrs. Weller to come up to the house. He replied that he did not know whether she, Mrs. Eddy, could see her. To this Mrs. Eddy said that she would like to have her come up. She could give her fifteen or twenty minutes—that would answer. She said, "I will send down and have her come up this afternoon." She added, "Mrs. Weller has written me two or three times for an interview, but it has always been so that I could not grant it, but now I can." Mrs. Weller was one of Mrs. Eddy's students.

Pleasant View, Concord, N.H.
Jan. 7

My dear friend,

You can have your same book, Christ and Christmas, any time. I am bringing out this edition in black ink the same as the first.

Be sure and let no one hear from you that your figures were

characterizing me in any way. The *gossips* are handling this to the injury of our Cause.

> Most truly,
> M B G Eddy

Mr. James F. Gilman
Dear Brother in Truth,—
　Mrs. Eddy wished me to return your book with her thanks, and say she will not need it for the next edition will be in black and she will have one of those.

> Very sincerely in Truth,
> Laura F. Sargent

TUESDAY, JANUARY 9, 1894

I sent Mrs. Eddy the following note:

> Dear spiritual Mother,
>　Yours is duly received, also the book, for which please accept my thanks. I am glad to have it to refer to, as new thoughts concerning it arise to occasion it, as I have sent the other for a week or two to a friend in Michigan.
>　Your article in the *Journal*[44] is wonderfully suggestive and is an able answer to the critics also. I have read and reread it a number of times. I think I can see plainly why it is that some should think the pictures "caricatures." It is because they are filled in mind with the materialistic art of today, the leading thought of which is *technical* accuracy and expression of the

merely human concept of things. The more I think of it, the more I see that the imperfections even, in the literal rendering, are a *help* to the real force of the pictures, because they are silent witnesses to the fact, all important, that the governing motive in their production was *spiritual purpose,* instead of the selfish one of trying to show personal ability. The pictures seem to say, "No doubt we make *material* mistakes, but we don't care if we do. What we want is that you shall see the wonderful beauty and power, and living vitality of the Christ as the Truth, the Way, as that which is "forever present, bounteous free," and "glows through gloom" even to the childlike in heart.

I resumed work on the portrait of the "Mother" last Thursday, and I am satisfied with the way I am now getting on with it. I think now that I shall have it ready for you to see by the last of this week, say Saturday P.M. or Monday. You will let me know when, after Saturday A.M. you would like me to come up. I do not expect to have the *literal* likeness done at that time, or in other ways to any more than *"approximate"* to my ideal, but perhaps it will be better that you see it and that will give me a new hold. I want to get it substantially right in everything but literal likeness, and ideal expression *first,* and then I shall be ready to carry out suggestions from Wisdom that I think will serve me well.

Very truly
James F. Gilman

I tell nobody anything.

Pleasant View, Concord, N.H.
Jan. 11 [1894]

Dear friend.

Thanks many for your apt criticism.

Please follow my directions once more. Stop all thinking about the work you have on hand, and wait before coming, to hear from me again. Turn your thought which way you will but not on your present work or on me.

Most truly,
M. B. G. Eddy

Pleasant View, Concord, N.H.
Jan 14 [1894]

Dear Bro. Gilman

It is of the utmost importance that you give this work yr immediate attention for we are in a hurry to print another edition of the book and Mr. Carlton has the other plates all ready printed and orders for books are pouring in rapidly.

Yr fraternally
C. A. Frye

The only change of plates in this edition of the book will be "The Way" so please finish *that first.*

FRIDAY, JANUARY 19, 1894

Mrs. Eddy wrote me day before yesterday that I could call upon her on Friday, so I went up at one o'clock. She soon came down into the library greeting me pleasantly and soon began talking about the portrait of her I was making. She said that she finds that she must give it up altogether. She said she would have Mr. Frye make me out a check for a hundred dollars to pay me for the time I had given to it. She seemed very pleasant about it and said it was in this just as it had been in everything she had undertaken. She said she might work and worry and change and fix, but it always had to be given up at last and then God's way could be carried out.

"And now," she said, "I must withdraw my illustrated poem from publication." She said, "It is with this just as with the closing of the college. There was a demand for the book that was fabulous. They never have been able to supply the books fast enough, and reports were coming in that it was healing the sick, and the report from judges on all sides was that the pictures were like the oldest of the old masters and everything seemed to point to its doing a grand work of good; and now it must be given up." She said, "It will not do to not heed the voice of God when it repeatedly called louder and louder." She said: "I turned to my *Science and Health* a short time since after this voice had been calling, and opened it at random, and this was what it was. And suiting action to her word, she reached for a copy of *Science and Health* lying on the table and began looking for the place. Not finding it easily, she got up and going to the hallway, she rang and asked Mrs. Sargent to bring down her *Science and Health*. She said to me, "I know just where it is in that one. I have a leaf turned down at the place." When it was brought, she began to read.[45]

This *Science and Health* appeared to be much used; a number of book marks were in it, and the corners of many leaves turned down. She read the extract to me to show me how pointedly the way was indicated that she walk in.

At the close of the interview she said to me, "Wait a minute while I see Mr. Frye." She went up stairs to find him. Soon she came back saying Mr. Frye was out, but she says, "I will have him write a check for you for $100 as I told you I would."

While talking about the illustrated poem and its success as a literary and artistic event, she said that a celebrated art critic of Boston had written of it for some periodical. I said I was beginning to get far enough from the work of helping bring it out to perceive some qualities in it not perceptible to me before, as others, outsiders, naturally view it. I said, "It is remarkable that the simple childlike qualities of the illustrations embodied in the simple loving motive to set forth the beautiful Christ ideal should have been evolved totally *without conscious intention* on the part of either of us. That was the very thing that made them the most valuable and artistic: self had been left out of them. And behold their beauty on that account." To this Mrs. Eddy responded by leaning forward in her chair toward me with an animated happy expression of agreement with what I was saying, and replying, "That is it! Self left out! The spiritual thought, male and female, working together. Oh! isn't it grand."

She said, "The illustrated poem is healing the sick and accomplishing great results apparently, but that it was through the *blind* faith and worship and not through understanding, which will not do. That is not the Christian Science idea. That is one reason why I must withdraw it."[46]

In speaking of obedience to God's voice—the importance of it—I said in reply to it, "We always, when we give up for sake of obedience, are given something vastly better than what we give up, according to my experience." "Yes, always," said she, "The reward of true obedience always more than satisfies us."

Speaking of the revising of *Science and Health* she said, "Over and over again I have written and rewritten until it had grown to whatever completeness it had now attained." This had been particularly so in her "spiritual interpretation of the Lord's Prayer," she said. "My efforts and wrestlings over this were beyond human conception. And in all these things no one could understand me. I was alone, and only God could understand." She often refers to this loneliness.

In February 1894 James Gilman moved to Gardner, Massachusetts, and he and H. E. Carlton, who had made the printing plates for *Christ and Christmas,* produced a book of scenes, *Pleasant View: The Home Surroundings of Mary Baker Eddy*. It was first published in August 1894. Two of Gilman's drawings, on pages 154 and 155, are from that publication.

—— 1895 ——

SATURDAY, AUGUST 9, 1895

Was at Mrs. Eddy's house to lunch in response to her kind invitation after getting some negatives completed for the book of scenes of Pleasant View, one being of Mrs. Eddy in her carriage just returning from her afternoon drive. At the table, referring to the excellence of some green corn that we had and which I think Mr. Frye said "The Professor" sent over, I inquired who "The Professor" was. The reply was that he was the principal of the Concord High School who had built a house opposite Mrs. Eddy's and was now grading the grounds. I had seen him at work himself with shovel and rake and supposed him a manual laboring man or at least not a scholar or professional man. I expressed something of this I think, as Mrs. Eddy replied in substance that he was one of the honest, straight-forward workers who took hold and demonstrated rather than preached.

She had talked with him on Christian Science ethics. She had

Photo by James F. Gilman

Mary Baker Eddy in her carriage on the drive in front of Pleasant View.
Calvin Frye handles the reins.

said to him, "You, as well as I, can remember when (and not so very long ago) everybody thought that they could not safely eat a hearty meal after three o'clock P.M. lest we suffer in consequence, but that now all this is changed. Six o'clock is the dinner hour and the heartiest meal of the day with many, with no evil consequences following or feared." She said he admitted that this was true.

After exchanging some expressions of thought upon the manifest tendency and seeming power of belief to manufacture laws of health, that governed us until we gave them up through necessity, I asked Mrs. Eddy the question: "Do you think that all mankind have got to pass through all this wilderness of belief in health laws, putting them to the test through dieting, exercise, fresh air, and so forth until their falsity being manifest, they should be ready to forsake them for the Truth, or have we about reached the climax now of this tendency toward materialism?"

At this she paused a moment as if gathering her energies for forcible expression, and then went on to say with vigor: "When the students of Christian Science practice what they preach, this climax of materialism will disappear and not before. Oh, the absurdity of preaching Christian Science and then not carrying it into daily life.

"Now, take the chiming of the bells at the new church in Boston. Why, I would no more have continued the chiming of those bells after I found that it was disturbing people, than I would have cut off my right hand. The Golden Rule would have guided them in this if they had been obedient to the Christian Science spirit. Divine Love never leads any to become obnoxious in that way."[47]

I said, "We who would follow you are apt to preach above what we can practice or are practicing."

She replied that in teaching we had to advocate or explain much above our practice, but we ought to be practicing all the time in whatever we have to do. "Oh, if others could only see what *I* see, how they would work and *strive* to express nothing but the spirit of Truth." She explained, because she sees these things and presses them upon students greatly—this necessity of practice in obedience to Truth—they often turn upon her with their darkness, thus making her burden greater and greater. She must consequently labor and watch lest this mark her thought and she reflect it upon them again. "I never have laid down any requirements until I have first suffered up to them," she said and appealed to Mr. Frye if he had ever known her to call others to the fulfillment of any requirements that she had not first herself suffered up to seeing their necessity.

"Oh," she said with great feeling, "it is not years that have whitened these hairs, but suffering, suffering from the dark thoughts of those whom I strive to bless, who turn upon me because I obey the Truth for their sakes."

She related that previous to the time when the chapter on "Marriage" was written she found that people were beginning to say of her doctrines that they were against marriage; that she was undermining the institution of the family; that her teachings led to the separation of husbands and wives and the breaking up of family relations, etc. This grew until it appeared such a great obstacle that it appeared to her a solid wall to her further progress. In this extremity, through its attendant suffering, she was impelled to the writing of the chapter on "Marriage," and when it came out, it was declared to be the best thing on "marriage" ever written. "It had its birth in the travail of soul that keenly sensed the need of the hour," she said.

Mrs. Eddy said to me, "I received your card indicating that you were practicing Science in Gardner. How do you get along in that?" I answered that I seemed to get along better in the healing when I had patients, than I did in explaining Science to people so that they would accept Science or ask for treatment. I added, "I seem to lack wisdom and tact in this, so that I have been without patients mostly this spring and summer and have taken up the art work in its place, keeping Science work in view as a leading thought."

She replied that my difficulty was a very common one. "Why, I have talked with M.D.'s when I was in Boston who had talked with my students and gained a wrong idea of what Science is. After I have explained the ideas a little, they would see and acknowledge the reasonableness of what I said and say they had before gained a very different idea of what Science is." I said, "Doubtless we try to explain the letter too much." "No," she said, "you do not explain the letter ever unless you are governed by wisdom. If you are talking with one who has not yet learned the A B Cs and trying to explain what is above and beyond the A B Cs do you *explain* anything to such? No, we need to practice this Science in whatever we are doing and this gives us the wisdom to talk to people what they can understand."

She said to me, "We should look to God and not inward for this help to right living. It is strange, when these things are explained to students as I explain them and they appear to understand them, that when they come to the matter of practice, all this is thrown or scattered to the winds, and they go on just the same as before."

I said, "That is just the way it is with me. I have an hour now and then when I see perfectly clear these scientific truths and the way to demonstrate them, and do demonstrate them for myself, but when I come to the testing with other people, all my perceptions are scattered and I seem to utterly fail." She said, "If you were abiding upon the Rock, this would not be so. You yet only have *gleams* of the Truth. You must get into the Truth all over and live in it." I said, "I do want to and I try to. Now, why can I not *do* it? I suppose I need to be more sternly resolved."

"No," she replied, "No, it is not human resolution, *but faith in God.* Having this faith, you would live it, for nothing can prevent it then. It is laziness among students that prevents their succeeding, just laziness. We must say to error, 'Get thee behind me, Satan.' We must *put it behind us;* by that *we put ourselves in front* of it, do we not? How *then* can it prevent or interfere with our progress in demonstration."

A short time after lunch, as I was out on the grounds briefly, giving some attention to sketching some details I needed in the next edition of the Pleasant View plates, word was sent out to me that Mrs. Eddy would like to see me at the house. Obeying the call, I found that Mrs. Eddy had an important message that she wished delivered to Judge Hanna[48] in Boston that evening and asked me if I would undertake to deliver it? Of course I was glad to be trusted to do it. She gave me money to meet my traveling expense, and finding Judge Hanna at his home on Commonwealth Avenue between 10 and 11 P.M., I delivered the message.

FRIDAY, AUGUST 15, 1895

I saw Mrs. Eddy this morning concerning the photograph of her sitting in her carriage. I now had a proof with me to show her for her approval. Mrs. Eddy liked it and approved of its being used for the new edition of Pleasant View pictures. She appeared very agreeable and in giving me her hand as I was about to depart for Gardner again, she expressed her good will saying, "God bless you."[49]

—— 1897 ——

During this year Mrs. Eddy and James Gilman collaborated on the reissue of *Christ and Christmas*. They made further changes in the art early in 1898. Because she was living in Concord, New Hampshire, and he in West Gardner, Massachusetts, their communication about the illustrations took place through the mail.

West Gardner, Mass.
April 6, 1897

Dear Mother: ——

I was at the Church in Boston on Sunday this week and visited "Mother's Room,"[50] the first time it has been my privilege to be there since Dedication. I think the window picture representing "the Mother" searching the Scripture is beautiful, tranquil and inspiring; and it is so much better with the face raised to the Light, than looking down as in "Christ and Christmas"—a change which I know must have been due to your thought or suggestion....

[The rest of his letter praises other stain glass windows in the Church and expresses gratitude for Mrs. Eddy's new book *Miscellaneous Writings*.]

> Very gratefully and
> affectionately your child
> in Christ,
> James F. Gilman

West Gardner, Mass.
April 17, 1897

Rev. Mary Baker Eddy
Beloved Mother

I have just forwarded to you by express a drawing of the Church in Boston from a hasty sketch made while I was in Boston two weeks since.—

Please accept as an Easter greeting from me, as a faint token of the gratitude I feel for the inestimable good thy Love bestows upon the world, and *me* daily. Oh, I do often thank the Eternal Good for the blessed presentment of the living God as the ever present potency and reality sufficient for the soul's aspirations for freedom from the thralldom of error, sin, and self. The reflections of Good from our precious new book,[51] and from the true and loving thought of brothers and sisters in Science make me feel how utterly unworthy self is to have any place in my thoughts and efforts in life.

> Sincerely and gratefully,
> Your child in Truth
> James F. Gilman

THE MOTHER CHURCH.

or

Prayer in Stone

The drawing that James F. Gilman sent to Mrs. Eddy. She wrote below it "or Prayer in Stone." The second and third buildings to the left of the church housed The Christian Science Publishing Society. The pool of water is fanciful. Mrs. Eddy ultimately gave the picture to The Christian Science Board of Directors.

Pleasant View, Concord, N.H.
April 19, 1897

My dear Mr. Gilman

Accept my thanks for your Easter gift. It is nicely executed and I will have it framed handsomely in memory of the giver.

Will you find time again to make over again the plate called "Christian Science" in "Christ and Christmas"? You nor I were never fully pleased with that and I have always meant to have it tried over. The position is not natural. Much detail will be required to make it suit me, and you have the idea of what is needed to express—so great a subject. Will you set about it soon so as to have it ready if I want to republish it at any future time?

Very truly,
Mary Baker Eddy

West Gardner
April 29, 1897

Beloved Mother,

In this redrawing of the illustration from *Christ and Christmas,* which I send this morning, I have sought to be governed by your Love and wisdom, to avoid extremes, and to keep what was good in the first picture, and add such improvement as the Spirit, through daily striving to obey has led me to feel was what you would have me try to do. Doubtless in this my obedience has not been complete, and you will see wherein my efforts have fallen short of the true ideal. The face and expression of the Healing Mother is such a delicate thing to have to do with that when what is in the picture I send appeared, I felt it might be right and I dared not meddle with it; and thought it best to wait until after you have seen it, and then if it appears not right I shall not be afraid to change it.

In this sacred work I do believe I have seen that the divine Love and Truth is *everything,* and obeyed alone enables us to do good and not evil. How grateful we should always be for your wonderful revelation of Christ—the Eternal changeless Good—to humanity.

Yours very truly,
James F. Gilman

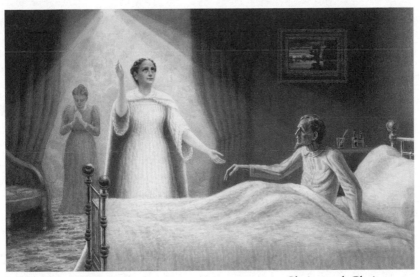

"Christian Science Healing" as it now appears in Christ and Christmas

Pleasant View, Concord, N.H.
April 30, 1897

Mr. Gilman
Christian Scientist,—
My dear friend,

Do you know what you have done for yourself, for mankind, for our cause? No, you do not perhaps but I will tell you. You have illustrated and interpreted my life on the plate that you sent me. Be sure that you do not in an unguarded moment *touch that face again*—remember this. Now my dear friend, do this. Let no mortal know about your success until you have crayoned that face and folded about the chest white drapery. Do not expose the neck, only about the throat, and that *not low*. Leave the arms and hands in the picture, that are facsimiles of mine 12 years ago, *only,* and have the neck round and full under the chin as mine used to be. If this is done and the face is not changed one iota in the process, your *fortune is made.* Take the picture of "Vesta" to guide you in draping. Else take the "Madonna" style that has nothing but the face that is seen. This is a matter of taste. You may have both or either to take to your work room till you select the style of one. All else but the figure of mine on the plate is to be left off or out of the picture that I project. The plate that you sent is just right for "Christ and Christmas."

If this is not known and no mind enters yours but the true thought, and its ideal, you will succeed to the end of what I propose. Be sure you keep silence and if you want a room here at Mr. Geo. H. Moore's, my cousin, on Warren street only when you *drape* and take my frames, you can get it by telling him Mother wants it so as to be hidden from observation.

> Ever Mother truly
> M B Eddy

P.S. I want to keep this picture and suppose you meant that I should. Oh I cannot let it go out of my keeping. I hope you have a duplicate to work from.

> Again Affectionately.
> M B E

Do not send a line on this subject by mail but by Express and see that the envelope is stitched and the Express is not paid by you leave that to me. *Obey* every word I say there is a reason for it all.

> M B E

West Gardner, Mass.
May 3, 1897

Rev. Mary Baker Eddy
My Dear Mother

Your dear letter of approval of my work has brought me gladness and spiritual comfort. My sorrow has been turned into joy and the infinite treasures and resources of divine Love and Truth appear anew giving me fresh hope and courage and confidence and perception of the right way.

It is the *spiritual perception* of your long suffering goodness that I *prize* the most. May that vision never be obscured whatever trials I may be called to endure, and I will ask no more, for with Love understood earthly self's insufficiency and weakness fades from view.

I will surely guard with "sacred secrecy" everything in connexion with this work committed to me as from God until it is accomplished and ready for its fulfillment, and I will strive more and more to appreciate the value and importance of the *true* thought uncontaminated by mortal mind which you in your great and wise Love have ever sought to impress upon me. Oh, I will strive to obey both the letter and the *spirit* of your commands for without that I have found I can do nothing.

I feel inadequate to the work you suggest. I must know it is God's work and my part is to keep out of God's way while I strive to fulfill His will—to silence mortal mind—self—and so keep my view of your purity, Truth and Love unobscured so I shall be governed by them and nothing else. "Spirit never repeats itself," never copies, but ever reproduces its own beauty of exhaustless Principle in *new* and fairer forms than before expressed, perhaps. Is not this the way? Mother's picture must be Love's picture or it will be no picture, and that must be fresh and *new*, direct from Spirit—from Principle—although it will be my duty to endeavor to make it like the one I sent you as nearly as I can, I will follow your directions. As to draping and detail that better be left until the last, until the face of Love has been given us.

Then I better go to Concord (or perhaps before). It is the *concord* of Soul that I need to visit for Light to show me the Way. I will see if I can find a "Vesta" here for suggestion as to draping. I have no doubt about the adequate handling of that after the face is expressed. Perhaps it may seem best to send that to you before I go to Concord for you to see when I feel I can safely do no more and before the draping is attempted. It may be some days before I am enabled to realize sufficiently the supremacy of Spirit to master the additional sense of error, sin, self—that threatens to beset me, but there I believe is where my work lies, for I am in blindness and weakness much of the time through mortal belief notwithstanding all efforts to the contrary.

Earnestly and hopefully
and gratefully Yours in Christ,
James F. Gilman

N.B. I will write again by Wednesday this week.[52] I begin work today and will seek only your constant spiritual approval.

J. F. G.

If I understood rightly, you desire the Light over the figure the same as in one sent you, also position of arms and hands and figure, although the rest in the picture I sent is to be left out.

West Gardner, Mass.
Oct. 14, 1897

Rev. Mrs. Eddy
Dear Mother

Christian Scientist[s] in Boston want to present the Christian Scientist[s] of Chicago at the time of their Church Dedication with a portrait. I told Mr. Bates[53] I was free to make one if I had your permission. Whereupon he asked me if I were willing to confer with you concerning this. He said one from the photo from which the picture in *Miscellaneous Writings* is made would answer made life size. Simply an accurate handmade crayon enlargement is what is in view. I told him the thought might find approval with you, and I write this accordingly. I will say that the artist's identity might be kept anonymous if that would help the case, or solve possible objections to the proposal.

Affectionately and gratefully
Yours for Christlikeness
James F. Gilman

DICTATED
Pleasant View, Concord, N.H.
October 15, 1897

Mr. Gilman
My dear Friend

I cannot recall my declaration not to have a portraiture of myself at present from any photo that I have on hand. This you may do if agreeable to the ones who want a crayon of me,—

bring out the beautiful plate in "Christ and Christmas" called *"Knocking"* and put underneath it the scriptural text "Behold I stand at the door and knock."

Omit the word that is on the plate in the book viz. "Knocking" and simply print the scriptural passage.

Most truly yours,
Mary Baker Eddy

Pleasant View, Concord, N.H.
Oct. 15, '97

To Mr. Gilman
My dear friend,

On "Knocking" Mr. Frye forgot to say that I want the inscriptions on the door and the scroll removed. The only fault with those plates in "Christ and Christmas" (that is conspicuous) is the inscriptions. But you and I know that people understand C.S. enough better now to permit this removal. Then they seemed to require labels to prevent their libels. I hope you will make a good thing out of it. May Heaven bless and angels guard you.

Most truly
Mary Baker Eddy

West Gardner, Mass.
Nov. 1, 1897

Rev. Mrs. Eddy
Dear Mother,

I have substancially completed the picture, "Knocking" such as is. In size it is about 28 x 36 inches inclusive of 4 inch margin all around it. Shall I send it to you for your inspection and approval, or will a plate from it by Mr. Carlton of the size of the one in *Christ and Christmas* be sufficient?—or shall I send both? I have felt limited in the execution to about what is expressed in the plate I have made it from. I hope what I have tried to do will be found acceptable to the righteousness and Truth I have sought to obey and follow in this work, but it is so easy to be self-deceived and misled by mortal mind if not thoroughly on guard against it that I do not feel to boast, or to be sure at all that I have achieved much.

> Lovingly Yours in Truth
> James F. Gilman

> Pleasant View, Concord, N.H.
> Nov. 2, '97

Dear Bro. Gilman

Your letter to Mrs. Eddy was duly received by her; in reply she thanks you and says, "Do not send either pictures, I have no chance to correct the drawing, even if it should need it, and I will trust you for the results. It should be *par excellence.*"

> Yours fraternally
> C. A. Frye

> West Gardner, Mass.
> Nov. 19, 1897

Rev. Mrs. Eddy
Dear Mother

I forwarded two photographic prints by Express this morning on 8:15 train of the picture "Knocking," sent ... a light and a darker one. I trust you will like them as well as the original one I made for you. Mr. Carlton made the negative at my request, as a precaution on my part against possible loss of the original in transit … and to be able in case you desired it to supply you a duplicate of the size of "Christ and Christmas."

Truly Yours, in the hope that the picture will prove of value in the Cause of Good and Christian Science.

James F. Gilman

Pleasant View, Concord, N.H.
Nov. 22, '97

To Mr. Gilman
My dear friend.

Your excellent letter breathing your pure faith in Divine direction gives me much pleasure.

Make the changes where ever you think best. God governing your thought is a sure pretext of success. Certainly put the scripture quote in its proper place at bottom of picture if my language was not thus, as it evidently was not. I [would] send the original picture but pray that you do not allow it to be defaced by travel. I fear Mr. Frye may not pack it properly.

With love mother
M B E

P.S. The aforesaid picture is framed and on the walls in my library. Mr. Frye advises your trying it with a print without sending the original. Please do this.

M B E

"Truth versus *Error" as it now is in* Christ and Christmas

Pleasant View, Concord, N.H.
Nov. 22, 1897

Dear friend

Please alter the plate "Knocking" that is now in "Christ and Christmas" thus. Make the door like the new plate. Leave the lettering off of scroll. Make the door plate *prettier.* Leave the window as it now is. Put on it the scriptural quotation you have with the new plate. Behold I stand etc.

Very truly
M B Eddy

To Mr. Gilman

Pleasant View, Concord, N.H.
Dec. 21, 1897

My dear friend.

Please attend at once to these changes in plates "Christian Science Healing" and "The Way." Make the hands of the healer the one pointing upward more distinct and both with fingers not quite as long and more in proportion to the hand. Also make that poor sick fellow's hand a hand not claw. Let it be thin but not so *long*.

Take the uprising figure out of its *bee-hive!*[54] remove the outlines of the plate and let it look as if outdoors.

I almost again hear you laugh as in the old way when we worked together over those plates.

Please accept a "Christ and Christmas" mailed with this.

Most truly yours
Mary Baker Eddy

May God bless thee this Christmas and every day and every hour of this and every year.

Mother

—— 1898 ——

West Gardner, Mass.
Jan. 10, 1898

Rev. Mrs. Eddy
Beloved Mother,

I have the pictures substancially done and expect to be able to Express you proofs tomorrow night so you will get them

Wednesday. The material elements have seemed to contend against progress in this work in a remarkable degree. I was kept waiting a whole week for needed material from Boston. After writing twice and waiting four days I went myself and then had to wait two days more. O it is lack of demonstration on my part I know. I do not awake to the probable need of the hour, but afterwards I see when it is too late to help matters. I only hope I have not failed also in the pictures. Violent teethache first one side, then the other is not a very fine accompaniment to putting delicate touches on pictures illustrating the supremacy of Mind over matter and pain. The inconsistency is so glaring that I hang my head with shame, professing as I do to being a Christian Scientist. But I am determined not to hide the error by keeping still about it. I have called patiently on the Lord and I can only hope that the need of the hour is that "Patience must have her perfect work."

> Truly Yours in Love & Truth
> James F. Gilman

To Mr. Gilman

> Pleasant View, Concord, N.H.
> Jan. 13, 1898

My dear Artist

The small print is a trifle too large. The arm and hand needs to be slightly more distinct but the body not wholly seen. The cherubs are to be *eliminated*—Then it will pass. Oh James, I thank you for the plate "Christian Science Healing." Accept this trifle in token thereof.

The only suggestion for this plate is make the bust slightly less, and make the waist of the female form a little more *tapering*. Please find check for $50.00 fifty dollars.

With love mother
Mary Baker Eddy

Pleasant View, Concord, N.H.
Jan 14, 1898

Dear Bro Gilman

I returned this morning the package. Since sending it Mrs. Eddy has decided to remove the figure of Jesus entirely from the plate, and place the dove, which is above his head, above the cross; and to place a crown in the air, about where Jesus' head now is.

Yours fraternally
C. A. Frye

To James F. Gilman

Pleasant View, Concord, N.H.
Jan. 18, 1898

Dear Bro. Gilman,

The picture arrived and mother is delighted with it. She sends her love & says "Good boy!" I have forwarded it this p.m. to Mr. Carlton to print from.

Yr. fraternally
C. A. Frye

Pleasant View, Concord, N.H.
Jan. 19, 1898

Mr. James F. Gilman
My dear friend:—

The art of Science is but a higher spiritual suggestion that is not fully deliniated nor expressed but leaves the artist's thought and the thoughts of those that look on it more rarified.

Now I suggest this picture for you to draw that possesses my thought of "The Way." Make the ground cross the same size of the one already made and the earth and this cross dark and without flowers or birds. Then rise on an incline thus:

crown

cross

cross

and put the singing birds and the flowers and the Dove with an olive branch in its bill on the second cross and have this cross lighter in shade than the lower one and smaller. Make the crown still fainter in form but *distinct*. Put the top of it in line with the top of the plate, thus giving the thought that all matter disappears with the crown or *crowned thought*. Make the star's radiance less solid and blunt, outline it as a shimmer not a shower of light and suited to the upper skies that you have made much to my liking. Make the crown some larger than the one that is made.

With love mother
Mary Baker Eddy

Pleasant View, Concord, N.H.
Jan. 19

Dear Mr. Gilman

Mother fears that you may not quite get one item of her idea as conveyed in letter sent this morning. The incline indicated on sketch in that letter she meant to have represent *the pathway*.

Yours fraternally.
C. A. Frye

West Gardner, Mass.
Jan. 21, '98

Rev. Mrs. Eddy
Beloved Mother,

The handling of this new idea to express it adequately is more than I at first supposed. The possibilities are so great that call for a fine discrimination that I need another day to work upon this, *and to think*—I will try and send it tomorrow noon, but perhaps it may seem best to keep it over Sunday.

The explanatory item sent me yesterday was needed and it immediately enlarged the scope of the picture as "The Way." My picture now expresses looking up the straight and narrow way to the crown, which way begins in the dark foreground and rises to the second, and lighter, and flower covered cross near the edge of the clouds and continues on to the crown at the top of picture. The perspective of this pathway causes the crown to look *very large* although it tis but little larger than the other on the paper.

I will make a great effort to send it tomorrow noon. I hope I have made the most of this without being extravagant, but I

"The Way" as it now appears in
Christ and Christmas

cannot tell but you can as soon as you see it. I have applied myself to this very closely and have sought God's help.

Truly Yours in Love
James F. Gilman

Pleasant View, Concord, N.H.
Jan. 27, '98.

Mr. Gilman
My dear friend.

Oh what a trial of my faith it is to continue to tell you just what to delineate and you put aside my directions and take your own devious course.

I told you to have the star give a shimmer of light, but you left it out altogether! I told you to have the crown in upper air where the sense of matter faded out. But you put clouds on the scale with Heaven where the crown should rest in thought above all pain, all sorrow, and "no night there." Your path is *no path* and your sky (if I can tell where it begins) looks like fish scales.

You seldom give my spiritual thought as I portray it, but will add your own material thought that utterly defaces it. This edition of my book is spoiled by this devious line of action,—the old Adam that insists on evil accompanying Good.

Now make one more plate-picture according to my directions already in your hands, and if you deviate in the least (only in failing to fairly delineate what I give for the model) but introduce either baby-faces, clouds, or tadpoles into Heaven's portals—then I am done with you.

With love mother
Mary Baker Eddy

Jan. 27, 1898

Dear Bro. Gilman

Mother forgot to say that there is a disproportion of size of objects in your picture of "The Way."

The birds are so small that they could not be seen as singing, and the olive branch in the dove's bill has no resemblance to leaves and there is too great difference in size of the 2 crosses.

Fraternally.
C. A. Frye

West Gardner, Mass.
Jan. 31st, 1898

Rev. Mrs. Eddy
Beloved and longsuffering Mother,

Your instructions so far as I can perceive make no further reference to landscape than what I have sought to express in this picture of "The Way." You wrote that the "sky was much to your liking" as in the picture when you wrote me the instructions, and so I have retained the lower clouds of that picture much the same. I feel that I shall need further instructions or light before I can do any more on this picture and so I send it as it is to that end. Please accept my gratitude for your *Love*.

Truly Yours,
James F. Gilman

Pleasant View, Concord, N.H.
Feb. 1, 1898

My precious student.

Seeking the light you will find it. I am satisfied with your progressive plate, for the present. Your thought has taken in much more of "The Way" than ever before. God grant that the burden becomes light and the way plain to you. Mother tried to break the cloud of sense in her last letter to you, and it did make it thinner so that the true idea shone through it. I thank you.

With love.
Mary Baker Eddy

The contacts between Mary Baker Eddy and James F. Gilman soon ended. While each of them moved ahead in their respective fields of labor and accomplishment, *Christ and Christmas* remains an enduring legacy of their unique collaboration.

An Album of
James F. Gilman's Art

SUNSHINE, SUMAC & SWEET-FERN   J. F. [illegible]

"Sunshine, Sumac and Sweet-fern"

"Landscape, New Salem, Ma."

"The Sentinel Tree, Athol, Ma."

"The Sentinel Tree, Athol, Ma."

The Sentinel Tree, an American elm then about 200 years old, can be seen on the distant hillside. The artist depicted this scene in various media. The larger of these two versions is pastel on canvas. The smaller, which has added to it an automobile and a streetcar, is rendered in gouache (opaque watercolor).

"The Mark Baker Homestead, Bow, New Hampshire, about 1830"
An imagined view of the childhood home of Mary Baker Eddy

"Dawn at Lynn, Lynn, Mass."

An imaginative presentation of the town of Lynn about the time Mrs. Eddy discovered Christian Science

"Pioneer Days in Christian Science, Orange, Ma."
The bearded man in the foreground is probably James F. Gilman.

When Mrs. Eddy withdrew her book *Christ and Christmas* from publication, she wrote this article for the February 1894 *Christian Science Journal* telling about her decision. She later included the article in her book *Miscellaneous Writings.*

Deification of Personality

by Mary Baker Eddy

*N*OTWITHSTANDING THE rapid sale already of two editions of "Christ and Christmas," and many orders on hand, I have thought best to stop its publication.

In this revolutionary religious period, the increasing inquiry of mankind as to Christianity and its unity—and above all, God's love opening the eyes of the blind—is fast fitting all minds for the proper reception of Christian Science healing.

But I must stand on this absolute basis of Christian Science; namely, Cast not pearls before the unprepared thought. Idolatry is an easily-besetting sin of all peoples. The apostle saith, "Little children, keep yourselves from idols."

The illustrations were not intended for a golden calf, at which the sick may look and be healed. Christian Scientists should beware of unseen snares, and adhere to the divine

Principle and rules for demonstration. They must guard against the deification of finite personality. Every human thought must turn instinctively to the divine Mind as its sole centre and intelligence. Until this be done, man will never be found harmonious and immortal.

Whosoever looks to me personally for his health or holiness, mistakes. He that by reason of human love or hatred or any other cause clings to my material personality, greatly errs, stops his own progress, and loses the path to health, happiness, and heaven. The Scriptures and Christian Science reveal "the way," and personal revelators will take their proper place in history, but will not be deified.

Advanced scientific students are ready for "Christ and Christmas;" but those are a minority of its readers, and even they know its practicality only by healing the sick on its divine Principle. In the words of the prophet, "Hear, O Israel: The Lord our God is one Lord."

Friends, strangers, and Christian Scientists, I thank you, each and all, for your liberal patronage and scholarly, artistic, and scientific notices of my book. This little messenger has done its work, fulfilled its mission, retired with honor (and mayhap taught me more than it has others), only to reappear in due season. The knowledge that I have gleaned from its fruitage is, that intensely contemplating personality impedes spiritual growth; even as holding in mind the consciousness of disease prevents the recovery of the sick.

Christian Science is taught through its divine Principle, which is invisible to corporeal sense. A material human likeness is the antipode of man in the image and likeness of God.

Hence, a finite person is not the model for a metaphysician. I earnestly advise all Christian Scientists to remove from their observation or study the personal sense of any one, and not to dwell in thought upon their own or others' corporeality, either as good or evil.

According to Christian Science, material personality is an error in premise, and must result in erroneous conclusions. All will agree with me that material portraiture often fails to express even mortal man, and this declares its unfitness for fable or fact to build upon.

The face of Jesus has uniformly been so unnaturally delineated that it has turned many from the true contemplation of his character. He advances most in divine Science who meditates most on infinite spiritual substance and intelligence. Experience proves this true. Pondering on the finite personality of Jesus, the son of man, is not the channel through which we reach the Christ, or Son of God, the true idea of man's divine Principle.

I warn students against falling into the error of anti-Christ. The consciousness of corporeality, and whatever is connected therewith, must be outgrown. Corporeal falsities include all obstacles to health, holiness, and heaven. Man's individual life is infinitely above a bodily form of existence, and the human concept antagonizes the divine. "Science and Health with Key to the Scriptures," on page 229, third and fourth paragraphs, elucidates this topic.[1]

My Christmas poem and its illustrations are not a textbook. Scientists sometimes take things too intensely. Let them soberly adhere to the Bible and Science and Health, which contain all and much more than they have yet learned. We should prohibit ourselves the childish pleasure of studying Truth through the senses, for this is neither the intent of my works nor possible in Science.

Even the teachings of Jesus would be misused by substituting personality for the Christ, or the impersonal form of Truth, amplified in this age by the discovery of Christian Science. To impersonalize scientifically the material sense of existence—rather than cling to personality—is the lesson of to-day.

Photogravure Reproduction

THE FIRST EDITION OF
Christ and Christmas was a handsome volume with the cover
gold-embossed, the endpapers patterned, the edge of the pages
tipped in gold, and sheets of tissue protecting the drawings.

The book had been printed in two stages and at two places.
First the art was reproduced in Gardner, Massachusetts, at the
printing shop of H. E. Carlton. Then these pages were delivered
to Edward N. Pearson at the publishing arm of the *Concord
Monitor* in Concord, New Hampshire, who saw to printing the
type and assembling the pages.

Carlton, acknowledged as photograveur in the original vol-
ume, used a "gelatine" process—photogravure—a method
barely fifteen years old. Especially good for printing the art in
Christ and Christmas, photogravure produces velvety blacks and
a full range of grays from silvery to midnight.

The process involves photographing the piece of art, develop-
ing the negative, making a positive from it, and then exposing a
gelatin-coated sheet of tissue through that. The gelatin hardens
in proportion to the amount of light reaching it. Thus the light-
colored areas of a picture harden the most; the darker parts, the

least; and the in-between shades do so in proportion to their depth of color.

The gelatin sheet is applied to a hard flat plate or cylinder. When washed in warm water, the areas of gelatin are washed away according to their softness. Thus the darker the original tone, the less gelatin remains; the lighter, the more. Now the design that has been transferred to the plate by the presence and absence of the gelatin is chemically etched into the plate. This time the darker the color, the greater the depth of design; the lighter the color, the less the depth.

The plates made for the art in *Christ and Christmas* are glass, a medium no longer used.

One of the glass photogravure plates prepared for the
first edition of Christ and Christmas.

Ready for printing, the plate is bathed in a thin and fast-drying ink and then wiped off with a blade, so that ink stays in the different levels of the incised design but not on the surface. Paper pressed onto the plate results in a print with a wide range of rich tones that are close to the tones of the original art.

When the book *Christ and Christmas* was ready, those glass plates—that photogravure printing—meant art handsomely reproduced.

A List of Illustrations in Christ and Christmas

1. "Star of Bethlehem," also called "Chaos"

2. "Christ Healing," also called "Christ-cure"

3. "Seeking and Finding," also called "candlelighted picture," "candlelit woman," "fierce heartbeats," "woman and serpent"

4. "Christmas Eve," also called "Christmas Tree"

5. "Christmas Morn"

6. "Christian Science Healing," also called "Christian Science," "Woman healing the sick," "Healing the sick"

7. "I thank thee, O Father, Lord of heaven and earth, because thou hast hid these things from the wise and prudent, and hast revealed them unto babes. —*Christ Jesus*"

8. "Treating the Sick"

9. "Christian Unity," also called "Unity," "Christ and Woman"

10. "Truth *versus* Error," also called "Knocking"

11. "The Way," replaced an original drawing that was also known as the "Ascension"

The art for *Christ and Christmas* is mixed media—primarily charcoal and wash, but with some pen and ink, and pencil.

The Letters from Pleasant View

MOST OF THE LETTERS in this book from Mrs. Eddy and members of her household to James Gilman have not been published before. They are part of the archival collection of the Church History Department of The Mother Church, and each one is identified by a Church History Document number. The dates and document numbers of these letters follow:

JAMES F. GILMAN

Letter of November 19, [1895]; Church History document L05724.

"YOU SEE I AM NOW IN CONCORD, N.H."

Letter of January 9, 1893; Church History document L02283.
Letter of January 23, 1893; Church History document L02284.

"A MATTER OF BUSINESS IN YOUR LINE"

Letter of March 8, 1893, (Calvin Frye); Church History document L06313.
Letter of March 10, 1893, (Calvin Frye); Church History document L06314.

Letter of March 20, 1893; Church History document Lo2285.

Letter of March 21, 1893; Church History document Lo6315.

Letter of March 28, 1893, (Calvin Frye); Church History document Lo6316.

Letter of March 30, 1893, (Calvin Frye); Church History document Lo6317.

Letter one of April 10, 1893, (Calvin Frye); Church History document Lo6318A.

Letter two of April 10, 1893, (Calvin Frye); Church History document Lo6318B.

Letter of April 14, [1893]; Church History document Lo2286.

Letter of [April] 15, [1893]; Church History document Lo2299.

Letter of April 23, 1893, (Calvin Frye); Church History document Lo6319.

Letter of May 5, 1893; Church History document Lo2287.

Letter of May 8, 1893; Church History document Lo2288.

Letter of May 8, 1893; Church History document Lo2289.

Letter of May 13, [1893]; Church History document Lo2290.

Letter of June 9, 1893; Church History document Lo2293.

Letter of June 17, 1893; Church History document Lo2294.

Letter of June 22, 1893; Church History document Lo2295.

Letter of June, 1893; Church History document Lo2292.

Letter of July 7, 1893; Church History document Lo2296.

Letter [July 1893]; Church History document Lo2298.

Letter of August 22 [1893]; Church History document Lo2301.

Letter of August 25 [1893]; Church History document Lo2302.

Letter one of September 1, 1893; Church History document Lo2303.

Letter two of September [1, 1893]; Church History document Lo8573.

Letter of September 7 [1893]; Church History document
    L02304.
Letter of September 25, [1893], Church History document
    L02305.
Letter of November 5 [1893]; Church History document
    L02306.
Letter of November 6, '93; Church History document L01266.
Letter of November 7, [1893]; Church History document
    L02307.
Letter of [November] 28, [1893]; Church History document
    L02308.
Letter of December 4 [1893]; Church History document
    L02309.
Letter of December 6, [1893]; Church History document
    L02310.
Letter of December 8, 1893; Church History document
    L02311.
Excerpt from letter of December 18, [1893]; Church History
    document L02312.
Letter of January 7, [1894]; Church History document L02313.
Letter of January [1894], (Laura Sargent); Church History
    document L06322.
Letter of January 11, [1894]; Church History document
    L02314.
Letter of January 14, [1894], (Calvin Frye); Church History
    document L06323.
Letter of April 18, 1897; Church History document L02328.
Letter of April 30, 1897; Church History document L02338.
Letter of October 15, 1897; Church History document L02330.
Letter of October 15, 1897; Church History document L02329.

Letter of November 2, 1897; Church History document
L06326.

Letter of November 22, 1897; Church History document
L02331.

Letter of November 22, 1897; Church History document
L02332.

Letter of December 21, 1897; Church History document
L02333.

Letter of January 13, 1898; Church History document L02334.

Letter of January 14, 1898, (Calvin Frye); Church History
document L06328.

Letter of January 18, 1898, (Calvin Frye); Church History
document L06329.

Letter of January 19, 1898; Church History document L02335.

Letter of January 19, 1898, (Calvin Frye); Church History
document L06330.

Letter of January 27, 1898; Church History document L02336.

Letter of January 27, 1898, (Calvin Frye); Church History
document L06331.

Letter of February 1, 1898; Church History document L02337.

APPENDIX FIVE

Art of James F. Gilman

page 12   "Montpelier, Vermont," 5¼" by 9", etching, 1889

page 13   "Winter's Day in Montpelier, Vt.," 4" by 7¾", etching, 1888

pages 24–25   "Pleasant View from the South," 6½" by 24", monochrome watercolor, photogravure reproduction, 1892

pages 26–27   "Pleasant View," 9" by 24", monochrome watercolor, photogravure reproduction, 1892

page 27   Enlargement of "Pleasant View"

page 32   "Mary Baker Eddy," 21½" by 17½", Conté crayon after H. G. Smith 1886 photograph, 1892

page 91   "Christian Science Healing," 12" by 18", primarily charcoal and wash, an original work for *Christ and Christmas,* 1893

page 95   "Truth *versus* Error," 26" by 32", primarily charcoal and wash, an original work for *Christ and Christmas,* 1893 page 103   "Christmas Morn," 12¾" by 17½", primarily charcoal and wash, 1893

page 127   "The Way," primarily charcoal and wash, 1893, also called "The Ascension"

pages 154–155 "View Looking Southward from the Verandah," 3⅜" by 9", photogravure reproduction, published in *Pleasant View: The Home Surroundings of Mary Baker Eddy,* 1894

pages 154–155 "The Pond (Evening)," 3¼" by 8½" photogravure reproduction, published in *Pleasant View: The Home Surroundings of Mary Baker Eddy,* 1894

page 187   "The Mother Church," 7" by 11¼", photogravure, 1898. "Or Prayer in Stone" added in handwriting by Mrs. Eddy

page 189   "Christian Science Healing," 12" by 18", primarily charcoal and wash, with changes made in 1897

page 197   "Truth *versus* Error," 17½" by 23½", primarily charcoal and wash, with changes made in 1897

page 203   "The Way," 10" by 15", primarily charcoal and wash, new illustration for *Christ and Christmas,* 1898

page 208   "Sunshine, Sumac and Sweet-fern," 15½" by 25¾", watercolor, tempera, 1905

page 209   "Landscape, New Salem, Ma.," 18" by 32", pastel on canvas, 1913 page 210   "The Sentinel Tree, Athol, Ma.," 18" by 32", pastel on canvas, 1913

page 211   "The Sentinel Tree, Athol, Ma.," 9⅜" by 16", gouache (opaque watercolor), 1912

page 212   "The Mark Baker Homestead, Bow, New Hampshire, about 1830," 16" by 20¾", charcoal, pencil, pastel

page 213   "Dawn at Lynn, Lynn, Mass.," 21½" by 37", oil on canvas, 1903

page 214   "Pioneer Days in Christian Science, Orange, Ma.," 6¾" by 12¼", lithograph, no date

This article, published in the 1891 *Christian Science Journal*, is written from an artist's viewpoint.

Backgrounds
by James F. Gilman

Not long ago I was present in the studio of a painter, and became very much interested in the subject: Use, and mission of backgrounds. The painter showed me, among other pictures, some partially executed ones upon which he was at work. One of these in particular engaged my serious attention, because of its deep shades and sombre tones, which suggested, rather than expressed in actual form, many indefinite things; for it was vague and shadowy; its leading features manifested only by graduated tones, that blended one thing with another in a way that made all seem to be clothed in, or not yet emerged from, a chaos of nothingness, which, while it continually attracted by what it suggested, left no satisfaction of definite idea in the beholder's thought. The artist told me that this was but the background, or preparation, upon which he proposed to set forth an ideal of beauty, still in his thought, which he considered one of his best conceptions; and asked me to come in again in a few days and see the completed picture, saying,—"A demonstration is better than a wordy description, which, in the absence of the accomplished work, leaves no impressions of value upon the mind."

My attention, at this time, was also called to another small painting which was shown me. "A study from nature," the artist called it, which, while it appeared interesting in many ways, still seemed of comparatively small importance. It was a landscape; some large trees were in it; a running brook, a road, and small bridge; some mountains in the distance; all of it bathed in every-day, common-place sunshine.

Awhile after, I was in the studio again, and was shown the completed picture, the background of which engaged my attention before, and, indeed, there had been a great transformation. The same background was there,—there could be no question about that, when it came to be considered and sought for,—but now it seemed to have a place and use in its complete subordination to the beauty and truth set forth upon it. But what seemed scarcely possible, the substance of the picture was the very same as the study from nature that had so lightly engaged my attention before. There were the same trees, the same running brook, the same sunlight; but *now,* how changed and glorious it all looked! How welcome looked the bright greens of the foliage, and the grass in the shining light! The brook sparkled with crystal purity, the variegated foreground was rich in tones of golden radiance in the detail of every-day things, *common and simple* things; and yet, now it was so attractive and comfortable to the eye that to leave it caused regret. Was all this in the study from nature also? Yes; but in the study, the sunlight and truth is everywhere, in all parts of the picture, with equal force; in the completed picture its *definite* appearance is mainly in the foreground.

The artist explained that the substance of the ideal was all indicated in the study, which was a literal, careful transcript from nature; but, until our eyes become sensitive by the growth and exercise of mind, we do not behold the ideal beauty of truth until it is separated, and thus relieved from, and by, its opposite absence in the background of the same picture.

He further explained that simple blackness, or whiteness was not sufficient in a background. It must be full of *graduated* tones, which only *suggest* many things of truth, and blend all its features in a common appearance of almost nothingness, which *separates* the *somethingness* of the ideal (which, by the way, is not *in* nature, but in the mind only) from the nothingness, and makes it, in that way, appear in the full and real power of its glory.

That the ideal is not in nature is proved by the photograph, which, more like this study from nature, gives us the absolutely accurate letter of form and detail, but misses completely the something we all love in the artist's picture. That something is *soul.* It is the *soul* of things that charms, and alone engages our real attention. It is the *spirit* of Truth—of light, form, color— that is the beauty that interests us long; *but this is expressed through mind only, and its conceptions.* Earthly or material forms or color often *suggest,* to our thought, our ideals, but they are not those ideals. If they were, a photograph of a scene would engage our permanent interest more perfectly than the most charming painting of the master could, because of its greater possible *literal* perfection.

It was mind that made the valuable and great pictures of the old masters what they are permanently. Why is this so, do you ask? Why is truth always so interesting, so attractive, so beautiful when we perceive it to be truth beyond question, so that even its simplicity becomes its crowning charm? From earliest memory, we all hate lies, injustice, wrong, when they appear as such to us; and correspondingly we all love the true, the real, the right. When our view of it does not conflict with notions that are from false idea begotten, which are contrary to it—of what *is* true, and real, and right.

In the early stages of our growth, truth always appears the more forcible when the ugliness of a lie, set forth as such in its garb of nothingness, is not far away, and that, I suppose, is why a background is a necessity to the forcible presentation of the beauty of truth in a picture, to most of us.

This idea of background, as a power to set forth and transform simple things of Truth into glorious things of worth, *to our eyes,*—which then appear, forcibly, as the real and valuable things that they always are, in Truth, to us when we perceive and understand them,—often has engaged my thought since, as I have remembered the frequency of dark shadows in this dream of mortal seeming, and considered the possible use, in some way, that they all, through Truth's omnipotent, all-searching law, will be *compelled* to serve, in future, to those whose picture of life they now are forming a dreary, somber part. May it not possibly be true, that in God's wonderful economy and wisdom, not a shade of sin, sickness, or death, but must, in due course, take its useful place of praise "to Him who doeth all things well," through its contrast of emptiness and shade?

We have observed, in the experiences of mortal life, that when a new light of understanding is given birth in thought and acceptance, darkness and gloom enshrouds, in varying degrees, the striving that is the travail of soul preceding all birth. When we consider the slightness, often of the outwardly apparent causes of important changes in life's aspect, it is easier to realize how all things are possible to Him who is Omniscient, and the Principle of all force and action.

As an illustration of the power of apparently slight causes, the courageous and persistent striving of the student with his difficult problem, who thus creates a vacuum or background of hardship in his thought, upon which the final perception of Truth appears by contrast, as joy and satisfaction that a new idea of understanding is born, is the type of the way of all advancement. Is it not by such new birth that the Kingdom of Heaven is gained, step by step, in God's strength? Is it not by such law that Truth's idea is gradually born into our sense of existence, always? Without the striving there is no gaining; without the hardship there is no joy; "No cross, no crown." If this be true, we may be sure no background is even in vain, or made so dreary that upon its face in due time shall not appear its opposite light and joy in proportionate sweetness.

Notes

THE SETTING

1. *Miscellaneous Writings,* 372.
2. *Ibid.,* 33.
3. *Retrospection and Introspection,* 24.
4. William Dana Orcutt, *Mary Baker Eddy and Her Books* (Boston: The Christian Science Publishing Society, 1950; renewed, 1978), 27, 61–62.
5. *Miscellaneous Writings,* 141.
6. *Ibid.,* 157.
7. In 1903 Mrs. Eddy asked students to cease from using the term *Mother* to designate her. In Article XXII, Section 1, of the *Church Manual* she requested that she be called *Leader.*
8. *Miscellaneous Writings,* 152.
9. *Ibid.,* 373.
10. *Ibid.,* 320. See also Revelation 22:16.
11. *We Knew Mary Baker Eddy* (Boston: The Christian Science Publishing Society, 1979), 97.
12. *Miscellaneous Writings,* 371.
13. Mary Baker Eddy to Carol Norton, December 14, 1893 (L02345).

JAMES F. GILMAN

1. A. A. Newhall, "Woburn Fifty Years Ago," *Woburn Advertiser,* 1882.
2. *Ibid.*

3. J. R. Greene, *James Franklin Gilman: The Man and the Artist* (Athol, Mass.: published in cooperation with the Athol Historical Society, 1996).

4. For information about the Vermont years, see Adele Godchaux Dawson, *James Franklin Gilman, Nineteenth Century Painter,* (Canaan, N. H.: Phoenix Publishing, 1975).

5. Dr. Richard Janson was director of the Robert Hall Fleming Museum, University of Vermont at Burlington.

"YOU SEE I AM NOW IN CONCORD, N.H."

1. Carrie Huse, a friend and correspondent of James F. Gilman, had moved from Vermont to Grand Rapids, Michigan.

2. Ebenezer J. Foster Eddy was a doctor of homeopathy before becoming a Christian Scientist and studying with Mrs. Eddy. She legally adopted him in 1888 to aid her in her work.

3. A student of Mrs. Eddy's, Ann Otis was sent by her to Concord, New Hampshire, in 1889 to introduce Christian Science there. She later served as a First Member of The Mother Church, before that function was abolished, and as a practitioner and teacher in Ann Arbor, Michigan.

4. S. A. Bowers was a photographer in Concord. (A photograph of Mrs. Eddy by Bowers is at the beginning of the chapter entitled "The Setting.") The two scenes of Pleasant View that Gilman drew for him appeared in the June 1893 issue of *The Christian Science Journal.*

5. About 137 to 165 yards.

6. Secretary is an inadequate description of Calvin Frye, for he also supervised Mrs. Eddy's household and grounds, kept her books, and was her aide and confidant for twenty-eight years.

7. She was actually seventy-one.

8. Mr. and Mrs. William Clark of Barre, Vermont. He studied with Mrs. Eddy in 1888 and later was a Christian Science practitioner and teacher in Barre.

9. A light afternoon meal or a more substantial early evening meal.

10. Mrs. Eddy wrote Foster Eddy the next day: "Last eve. I worked, and the dear Father's presence was with me and my 2 guests are sealed for the heaven of Soul, and one is snatched from the jaws of the Lion" (L01805).

11. " 'The way,' in the flesh, is the suffering which leads out of the flesh" (*Unity of Good*, 55).

12. The Columbian Exhibition, or 1893 Chicago World's Fair, considered by some authorities the greatest world's fair of all time, covered over 600 acres and ran from May through October. Christian Scientists had an exhibition there and participated in the auxiliary World's Parliament of Religions. Newspapers all over the United States gave considerable coverage to preparation for the fair as well as to the fair itself.

13. Republished in *Miscellaneous Writings*, 203–207. It was first published in *The Christian Science Journal* in August 1892.

14. Laura Sargent, Mrs. Eddy's companion and housekeeper, alternated these duties with her sister Victoria Sargent of Ocono, Wisconsin, and Clara Shannon of Toronto, Canada.

15. The Christian Scientist Association of the Massachusetts Metaphysical College was composed of students of Mrs. Eddy. As such, Laura Sargent would be at the meeting. "Obedience," the address Mrs. Eddy wrote especially for the meeting, was published in the March 1893 issue of the *Journal* and later reprinted in *Miscellaneous Writings*, 116–120.

16. "Its basis being a belief and this belief animal, in Science animal magnetism, mesmerism, or hypnotism is a mere negation, possessing neither intelligence, power, nor reality, and in sense it is an unreal concept of the so-called mortal mind" and "Man is properly self-governed only when he is guided rightly and governed by his Maker, divine Truth and Love" (*Science and Health*, 102, 106).

17. Mrs. Eddy established the Board of Education in 1898. The year

before—1897—she had stopped all teaching for one year following the publication of her book *Miscellaneous Writings*.

18. June 13, 1888, at the Central Music Hall.

19. See *Miscellaneous Writings*, 98.

20. Mary Baker Eddy, *Science and Health with Key to the Scriptures*, 452.

"A MATTER OF BUSINESS IN YOUR LINE"

1. James Gilman had done etchings of the Episcopal and other churches in Montpelier.

2. In recent years there had been defections of students and controversies about organization. Mrs. Eddy was also urging the start of construction of the church edifice.

3. An Episcopal clergyman and popular writer, Phillips Brooks was rector at Trinity Episcopal Church at Copley Square in Boston, Massachusetts.

4. Proverbs 3:5, 6.

5. Altered later by Mrs. Eddy to

> In tender mercy, Spirit sped
> A loyal ray
> To rouse the living, wake the dead,
> And point the Way—

6. Mrs. Eddy disapproved of this suggestion on April 8.

7. Altered later by Mrs. Eddy to

> The Christ-idea, God anoints—
> Of Truth and Life;
> The Way in Science He appoints,
> That stills all strife.

8. *Science and Health* by Mrs. Eddy.

9. At that time fledgling students of Christian Science in Concord were being influenced by Josephine Woodbury, a former student of Mrs. Eddy's. The actual target was Mrs. Eddy and her work. Gilman calls the effect on him depression, but Mrs. Eddy wrote Foster Eddy

that Gilman was kept "stirred up so that he cannot work half of his time" (Lo1863). Mrs. Woodbury's ultimate attack on Mrs. Eddy through the courts failed in 1901.

10. *Science and Health,* 118.

11. He read a weekly lesson that contained parallel references to the Bible and *Science and Health.* The topics of these lessons, which were published in a quarterly periodical, *The Christian Science Bible Lessons,* came from the International Sunday School Lessons used in Protestant churches. In 1898 Mrs. Eddy provided the twenty-six topics in use today.

12. Altered later by Mrs. Eddy to
> Truth pleads to-night: Just take Me in!
> No mass for Me!

13. Changed by Mrs. Eddy to
> What can rehearse the glorious worth
> Of his high morn?

14. "What I term *chemicalization* is the upheaval produced when immortal Truth is destroying erroneous mortal belief" (*Science and Health,* 401).

15. "The distant dome in this picture which I added for beauty's sake and thinking of the State House dome in Boston, appears at a later date to have been prophetic of the present Mother Church dome erected A.D. 1906" (James F. Gilman).

16. "Voices of Spring" republished in *Miscellaneous Writings,* 329.

17. Altered later by Mrs. Eddy to:
> O gentle presence, peace and joy and power;
> O Life divine, that owns each waiting hour,
> Thou Love that guards the nestling's faltering flight!
> Keep Thou my child on upward wing tonight.

18. The drawing "Truth *versus* Error."

19. "Christ Healing" which depicts Jesus raising the dead.

20. "Later in these records it is seen that the leaving off of my signature resulted in a much greater honor to me than the usual signature

without it would have been" (James F. Gilman). See entry for November 28, 1893.

21. Edward N. Pearson was manager of the printing operations of the *Concord Monitor.* He also became its editor.

22. "I have since seen that it was probably the financial storm and distress with the throwing out of work of thousands and riotous tendencies among the lawless unemployed &c. that she referred to as the work of malicious mind" (James Gilman).

23. J. M. Runnels had a store in downtown Concord, which also sold art supplies.

24. *Science and Health,* 247:21–24.

25. The son of Abraham Lincoln.

26. Martha Morgan was a student of Mrs. Eddy's. She and Calvin Frye were with Mrs. Eddy when she spent a month in Barre, Vermont, in 1889.

27. W. W. Brown was a photographer in Concord.

28. Emma Easton Newman. She tells of visiting Mrs. Eddy at Pleasant View in her article "The Primary Class of 1889 and Other Memories," in *We Knew Mary Baker Eddy* (Boston: The Christian Science Publishing Society, 1979), 93.

29. *Retrospection and Introspection,* first published in 1891.

30. Probably a foster father. When he was ten, James Gilman's mother died, and he and his siblings went to live with others. His natural father passed on in 1875.

31. A precaution to avoid communicating through the mails. It would later be discovered that her mail was being opened and read at the Concord Post Office.

32. H. E. Carlton lived in Gardner, Massachusetts. His firm did the reproductions of the art for *Christ and Christmas.* He and Gilman later published two books of photographs of Pleasant View.

33. Both in the telegram she sent and in a later letter, Mrs. Eddy asked Foster Eddy to return to Gardner. In the letter she wrote, "Please remain in Gardner until the artist gets the one thousand copies

finished which complete this edition of my work and then *bring them with you to me in* Concord" (L06284).

34. Edward A. Kimball was a Chicago student of Mrs. Eddy who was coordinating the Christian Scientists' participation in the World's Fair.

35. Judge Septimus J. Hanna, the Editor of *The Christian Science Journal,* would be reading Mrs. Eddy's paper at the World's Parliament of Religions in Chicago. He arrived in the afternoon and spent the night at Pleasant View.

36. In accordance with Mrs. Eddy's wishes and foresight these comments on her residence are applied to her first and last homes. Pleasant View was taken down in accordance with a codicil she appended to her will.

37. The Reverend Joseph Cook of Boston. A conservative religionist and opponent of Christian Science, he had some years before attacked Mrs. Eddy in the press and at one of his popular Monday lectures at Tremont Temple. Her reply can be found on page 95 of *Miscellaneous Writings,* "Christian Science in Tremont Temple."

38. In great contrast to Gilman's bucolic visit, later that afternoon Joseph Armstrong, William B. Johnson, and Ira O. Knapp—members of The Christian Science Board of Directors—would meet with Mrs. Eddy to discuss the start of the construction of The Mother Church edifice.

39. By 1910 the forms of the names had been changed to "Mary Baker Eddy and James F. Gilman," as they now appear.

40. When a teenager, Annie Dodge had been healed of an illness considered incurable in one prayerful treatment by Mrs. Eddy. She then studied with her, later serving as a practitioner in Denver, New York, London, and Washington.

41. Republished in *Miscellaneous Writings,* 116.

42. William G. Nixon served from August 1890 to January 1893 as publisher of Mrs. Eddy's writings. As one of three trustees holding the

church lot so The Mother Church edifice could be built, he strenuously disagreed with Mrs. Eddy's plans for her church.

43. Janette Weller was a practitioner in Boston.

44. "Christ and Christmas," *The Christian Science Journal,* January 1894. Reprinted in a slightly edited form in *Miscellaneous Writings,* 371–376.

45. There is no record of what Mrs. Eddy read to Gilman.

46. Mrs. Eddy wrote about her reasons for withdrawing *Christ and Christmas* from publication at that time in an article in the February 1894 *Journal.* It can be found in *Miscellaneous Writings,* 307–310, and is included in this book on page 215.

47. The chimes of the new Mother Church had been sounding every fifteen minutes, twenty-four hours a day. Mrs. Eddy learned of this and put a stop to it.

48. Judge Septimus J. Hanna was now First Reader of The Mother Church as well as the Editor of the *Journal.*

49. "This proved to be the last personal interview" (James F. Gilman).

50. Mrs. Eddy closed this room to visitors in 1909.

51. *Miscellaneous Writings.*

52. If he did send this letter, it is not extant.

53. Probably Edward P. Bates, a student of Mrs. Eddy's and a Trustee of The Christian Science Publishing Society. He would later serve for many years on The Christian Science Board of Directors.

54. The original drawing for "The Way," called also "The Ascension," was a rounded triangle, rather like the shape of a beehive. See p. 127.

APPENDIX ONE

1. See the revised edition of 1890, or page 334, lines 10–30 in current editions.

Index

P.114. healing a joy; teaching - suffering